The Roman Catholic Church

Its Origin and Nature

John F. O'Grady

PAULIST PRESS
New York / Mahwah, N.J.

Library of Congress Cataloging-in-Publication Data

O'Grady, John F.
    The Roman Catholic church : its origin and nature / John F. O'Grady.
        p.   cm.
    Includes bibliographical references.
    ISBN 0-8091-3740-2 (alk. paper)
    1. Catholic Church. I. Title.
BX1746.037
282—dc21   97-22380
                                                                                  CIP

Published by Paulist Press
997 Macarthur Boulevard
Mahwah, New Jersey 07430

Printed and bound in the
United States of America

Contents

■ Dedication ■

To all who love the Roman Catholic Church, especially
Carlo M. Martini, S.J., Cardinal Archbishop of Milan
Howard J. Hubbard, Bishop of Albany
Sr. Serena Branson, D.C.
Edward J. O'Grady
Joseph P. O'Grady
Patricia A. Borg

And the children, the future of the Church:
Bridget, Colleen, Christine, Alexander, Patrick, Colette,
Diana, Courtney, and John F., III

Preface

---

*T*he Roman Catholic Church exhausts any efforts to study or comprehend. The origins rest on faith and its continuation in history presupposes faith. Still, faith seeks understanding, and so this work joins in the efforts to understand. Like any effort in theology the result remains incomplete, waiting for others to use and go beyond.

The foundational document in this study of the Church, as in all I write, remains the Bible. I have also tried, however, to include the corresponding theological insights as well as the history that has transpired since the writing of the Bible. Much more could have been written on any topic covered, and many more topics could have been treated. I selected what I considered not only essential but also helpful for my audience.[1]

Questions that face the contemporary Church should be treated as well as origins of the Church. The Church will face them openly without fear, always seeking the truth.[2] Any study of the Church should also include the examination of Church structures dealing with such issues as equality, membership, governance and the relationship between clergy, religious and laity. In particular, the Petrine function and infallibility raise questions that seek greater clarification. Some of these issues cause an uneasiness for leaders of both the Church and the laity. This work will not solve the problems, but I hope a return to sources can help in seeking some resolutions by offering some general approaches and principles.

Pope John Paul II has warned against an historicism which equates truth with the perspective of an age. In the same speech[3] the pope also warned of those who "shut themselves up rigidly in a given period of the history of the Church and at a given moment of theological formulation or liturgical expression which they have absolutized...without considering history in its totality and its legitimate development." Somehow the Church must be like the scribe of Matthew who brings out the new and the old from the storeroom (Mt 13:52).

Most people realize that things in the Church today are not as they always have been. Thus the future need not just be the repetition of the past. Issues associated with ministry have always engendered intense discussion, even if today some additional topics have been added. The questions of married clergy, the celibacy of Roman Catholic priests, and the ordination of women will not go away. In all of these issues, the New Testament gives no clear answers but only suggestions toward a solution. Since this has been sufficient for two thousand years, it will have to suffice for the contemporary Church as well.

The role of the Church in politics and economic and social life has only recently begun to be explored. How the Church will function in these areas surely will differ from continent to continent and region to region. But the Church will make its contribution. To fail to do so would be to deny its origins in the teachings of Jesus.

Finally, the role of the Church as teacher in matters of personal and sexual morality needs careful examination. Too often the Church says too much, and then, too often, the world just ignores the Church. Certainly people need guidance in this troubled area of life, and the Church must find the way to offer guidance without losing credibility.

Personally, I feel comfortable in the Roman Catholic Church both as a priest and as a fellow believer. In an age when institutions seem to crumble too quickly, the Roman Catholic Church withstands even the worst of crimes and criticisms. This gives assurance for the future.

Over the past twenty years, my education, teaching and experience have enabled me to combine scriptural insights with systematic theological traditions and pastoral experience. During this period I have learned much from functioning as a parish priest in St. Matthew's Church, Voorheesville, New York, and from its two pastors, Rev. John A. Keefe and Rev. Arthur A. Toole. In Albany I have also benefited from the guidance of my first pastor, Rev. Msgr John L. Jones, and the pastoral insights of Rev. James D. Daley and Rev. Thomas J. Vail. I have also assisted at St. Patrick's Church, Wadsworth, Illinois, and learned much about the practical implications of scripture and theology from its pastor, the Rev. George J. Dyer. At St. Lucie's Church, Port St. Lucie, Florida, the people and their pastor, The Rev. Peter C. Dolan, welcomed me warmly. The people in these Roman Catholic parishes have listened to me and my interpretation of scripture. They have helped me to understand themselves as they live their lives as best they can as people of faith and as Roman Catholics. They also have helped me to understand the meaning of priesthood of all believers as well as priesthood of Order.

The students I have taught over the years, especially the graduate students, have also added to my practical understanding of needs and questions concerning the Church. I am particularly grateful to Alicia Marill who continues to teach me. They have all been believers, but not necessarily Roman Catholic. This has contributed significantly to my understanding of the Christian Church.

Above all, my living in Rome has shaped my awareness of what Roman Catholic means. Quickly I learned that the Catholic Church is Roman and more than Roman. The years in Rome live on in all that I do and write. Rome, with all its diverse meanings, has imprinted its traditions and its history on all those who have lived there.

This book is intended for a particular audience: Roman Catholics in the United States, interested adults, and college students. In the past my books have also been used for parish study groups with much success. I think this present work will find an accepting audience for these groups as well.

Throughout my life I have been blessed by knowing and learning from, and being friendly with, people on all levels of the life of the Roman Church. I have had the good fortune to know cardinals and archbishops and bishops and clergy and religious and thousands of wonderful men and women who share my faith. They are each part of me. I hope I remain part of them. We are all one in this one Church. This work is offered to the whole Church, but especially those who have committed themselves to the Roman Church. The various people singled out represent all the rest.

I continue to live and write in Florida, surely one of the most beautiful places on earth. Full of beauty and tragedy, this part of the world mirrors the Roman Church: good and evil, beautiful and ugly, truthful and false, but always God's great gift to humankind just as the mixture of goodness and evil in creation never destroys God's great gift.

June 29, 1996, Feast of Sts. Peter and Paul
Miami, Florida

Notes

1. The great lack in this book will be a thorough history of ecclesiology. Students should turn to general theological dictionaries and encyclopedias. In particular I would also recommend A. Dulles, "A Half Century of Ecclesiology," *Theological Studies,* Vol. 50 (1989), 419–442. Dulles examines the twenty-five years before the Vatican Council and the years 1965 to 1989. I am also personally convinced that no one can understand the Church in this century without understanding something of what happened in the nineteenth century. Some general work on this period would be helpful.

2. "If knowledge of the Church's history is essential to forming the Catholic Christian understanding, it goes without saying that the goal of the researcher must be the truth." J. Hennessey, "Grasping the Tradition: Reflections of a Church Historian," *Theological Studies,* Vol. 45 (1984), 159.

3. "Tensions of the Post-Conciliar Period," *Origins,* Vol. 10 (1980), 52.

■ PART I ■

Introduction

1.

Do We Need the Church?

---

*T*he very title of this chapter will of necessity cause the reader to pause, think and react, as fundamental questions arise that cut to the very heart of both history and theology: What do you mean by "Church"? What does "need" mean? Certainly for many Roman Catholics "the Church" means the Catholic Church of Rome.[1] But for millions of others, "church" means either the amalgamation of all Christian communities or their own particular denomination or even their own personal and local Christian community. "Need" will always be somewhat subjective.

Christianity contains various expressions of faith in Jesus that many find difficult to understand. The mainline churches are easy enough to identify. But what of the thousands of storefront churches in every city and town in the United States. What place do the evangelicals hold in this wider Christian community? What of the free and charismatic communities that seem to transcend all of the denominations, united by their participation in the one Spirit?

CHRISTIAN DENOMINATIONS

Mainline
Roman Catholic
Orthodox
Baptists
United Methodists
Lutheran
Presbyterian
Episcopalian

3

Mainline Smaller Communities
Congregationalists
Dutch Reformed
Quakers
Disciples of Christ
United Church of Christ

Evangelical Pentecostal

Storefront Churches

Any author must of necessity limit the scope of a study. Such limitation does not imply a disregard or a lessening of interests in other aspects of the phenomenon under examination. Rather, the very notion of Church is so vast and involves so many viewpoints and opinions that partial studies alone can best contribute to the broader understanding.

The question can then be asked in a twofold manner: Does society need the Roman Catholic Church and do individuals need the Roman Catholic Church? The study will focus on this particular Christian Church. Many of the ideas presented here, however, can be applied to other Christian communities. Any study of the New Testament, for example, offers a broader vista than that which is confined to Roman Catholicism. But many other aspects under consideration will refer primarily to the Roman Church.

Of all the Christian communities, the Roman Church, moreover, has the most complicated and yet most simplified mode of organization. The local church continues to hold a most important place for Roman Catholics. That means a parish and a diocese. They, however, also have a strong tie to the Church of Rome and its bishop, the pope. Even if the local church can function without complete guidance and control from Rome, the very presence of Rome and its perspective affects how the local church sees itself and how it manifests its understanding of the Jesus tradition. Even the traditions that have characterized the Roman Church for almost two thousand years have different applications in the local church. Somehow parish and diocese and Rome influence each other, with the parish influencing Rome the least and Rome influencing the parish the least.

ROMAN CATHOLIC STRUCTURE

Pope and world Church
Bishops and local dioceses
Pastors and parishes

■ **The Catholic Church and Society** ■

Historically, religions have functioned as a critique for the broader society. Religion can point out not only the presence or absence of God in any situation but also the presence or absence of care for human value and dignity. When a society tries to muzzle religion, people suffer. The example of the last fifty years in eastern Europe exemplifies this truism. Society needs religion to protect it from itself.

Since the emancipation by Constantine, the Roman Church has offered much to western culture. Surely over the past two thousand years many sins have been committed by Church people, often in the name of God and religion, but overall the contribution has been good.

All human rights have not always been in the forefront in the history of the Roman Church, but some human rights were always protected. Now the Roman Church expresses concern for all human rights of all peoples in all places and times. The buildup was slow. An institution of two thousand years acts slowly. At this moment in history, however, no one can doubt the contribution of the Roman Church to the development of human rights for all.

Some may quickly question the present situation of women today in the Roman Church. The present prohibition of ordination can well be construed as inimical to the rights of women. The past twenty years, however, have seen a remarkable change in the Roman Church with regard to women. Who knows what the next twenty years will bring?[2]

In culture, literature, art and learning, the Roman Church has excelled. Even the most jaded atheist or agnostic recognizes the contribution of the Roman Church to these fields of human accomplishment. Libraries, museums, even the origin of the university systems of the west, can be traced to the Roman Church. Here the Christian community coming from Rome has much to be proud of.

Over the past two thousand years, western culture in particular has benefited immensely from the Roman Church. Other cultures also have been enriched by this particular community. But still the question remains: Does society, did society, need the Roman Church?

Certainly human rights can develop outside the influence of Christianity and the Roman Church. Culture and learning can never be limited to a particular influence. The more sober response to the question would have to be: The Roman Catholic Church has perdured as a relative necessity to society and in particular to western culture. Surely western culture would be very different without the influence of the Roman Church over the past two thousand years, but even this would allow only a relative necessity for its contribution to the world.

■ The Individual and the Roman Catholic Church ■

Does the individual need the Roman Church? In a world in which less than thirty percent are Christians, the answer is easy: No. Even within the very traditional understanding of Jesus and his message the answer is no. Since God wills the salvation of all peoples, then Christianity, and even Roman Catholic Christianity, the largest of the communities following Jesus, must become relative to the salvation of the individual. God remains God, and if God so wills the salvation of all peoples, then Christianity must be the extraordinary means of salvation rather than the ordinary means of salvation. God must have other plans for the more than seventy percent of the world's population who do not claim to be followers of Jesus of Nazareth.

Sociologically, religion offers much to the individual. People tend to identify with groups. Individuals both offer and receive support from uniting with people of similar beliefs and faith. Most people need other people in their religious search. The Christian Church, and the Roman Church in particular, provides such support. People may not need a particular religious group, but in general most people need some religious grouping.

Psychologically, the same seems true. The community expression of faith allows for a deepening of trust and commitment to God and to others. People feel good within the context of a religious community. The uneasiness about the major questions in life lessens. Life can take on new meaning and happier expression through participation in some religious groupings. But again, this can be fulfilled by many such gatherings. Religion remains one such grouping among many.

Theologically, religion, no matter now helpful, never becomes an absolute necessity. If God offers a relationship to people, then this offer is first personal, intrinsic and transcendent before it ever becomes public, extrinsic and categorical in organized religions.[3] Any religious community only helps in the search for God in human life. Ultimately, however, it comes down to the individual seeking to discover and accept the presence of a mysterious force or power or being in the universe that gives foundation and meaning to human existence.

NEED OF RELIGION FOR THE INDIVIDUAL

Sociological: groups offer support
Psychological: helps people to feel good
Theological: helps in search for God

The necessity of the Roman Church for the individual further refines the question. For some, the Roman Church is not only necessary but an absolute necessity. Some people are so bound to this Church and its traditions that truly the thought of not being part of this Christian community becomes a practical impossibility, even if arguably a theoretical possibility. Many people need the Roman Church, for to be separated from this Church amounts to spiritual suicide.

Such a position surely does not prevail for all Roman Catholics by birth, education and even commitment. Often when circumstances change, these same individuals who were once even deeply committed to the Roman Church change allegiances. Usually the circumstances involve the very heart of the person's life and happiness. Marriage often can cause a change in commitment to Roman Catholicism. The same is true for divorced Roman Catholics who wish to remarry and cannot do so within the Roman Church.[4] Many Roman Catholic women have taken refuge in the Episcopal Church in the United States over women's ordination. For these, the necessity to be a Roman Catholic takes second place to other dimensions in life.

Society may not need the Church, but it helps. Every individual may not need the Church, but it helps. And most individuals need some form of organized religion. Society may not need the Roman Catholic Church, but the Church has probably done more good for society than any other organized religion. Does the individual need the Roman Catholic Church? Theologically, since God has willed to give us Jesus and has also offered us an inspired book, the Bible, the Church becomes a necessary part of the divine plan even if the Church never becomes an absolute necessity for every individual or for every society.

■ American Roman Catholics ■

Almost twenty-five percent of Americans are Roman Catholics. As a group they are serious-minded in most matters and, like their fellow Americans they want to enjoy the good life not only for themselves but for their children and their children's children. American Roman Catholics have become more and more assimilated to their other Christian denominational friends and acquaintances with regard to their religious practices. At the same time American Roman Catholics still retain a strong commitment to their local parish and diocese as well as to the bishop of Rome. These bonds form part of their personal understanding of God and religion and themselves. They are taken seriously even if more and more American Roman Catholics question many Church practices.

As a group, these same American Roman Catholics are well educated and committed to education for their children. They are curious and seek ever greater understanding. They have encouraged their children to continue intellectual pursuits as well as socioeconomic pursuits. They maintain a commitment to a long line of people of faith that they believe brings them right back to the time of Jesus and the earliest gathering of his followers. They feel secure in that tie with the past and feel confident that the same line will continue into the future. Their Church is Roman and Catholic and Christian. They may know that this Church can never be an absolute necessity for all peoples, but for them it is at least a relative necessity, and for many that necessity becomes absolute. They hope, with a guarded optimism, that their children will feel the same way about the Church. They pray that their grandchildren will continue the line of faith and commitment but always as American Catholics.

American Roman Catholics know that the Roman Church has its origins in the teaching of Jesus. The New Testament testifies to this community. Over the centuries this Church has understood itself as one, holy, Catholic and apostolic. It remains so. The Roman Catholic Church ministers to its own members and to the world community. It preaches the word of God to its members and makes

God present to them through Jesus and its sacramental system. This Church offers its service to the world community not only in what it has preserved from the past but in what it teaches today. The Church has become multinational and multicultural. It has embraced both rich and poor, educated and uneducated, developed peoples and developing peoples. It has withstood totalitarian regimes and flourished in democratic societies. It has sinned and been graced. The saint and the sinner have found shelter within its arms. The Roman Catholic Church has good and noble marks.

American Roman Catholics also know that their particular experience has affected their Church. A nation with a fierce commitment to freedom and individual rights not only has welcomed Roman Catholic traditions but also has shaped them. American virtues include forgiveness and generosity and acceptance of differences. Loyalty to parish, bishop and pope grows in the context of American history and American virtues. The Roman Catholic Church in the United States differs from the same Church in France or Italy or Eastern Europe. If the Roman Catholic Church has noble marks, so does the American Roman Catholic Church.

■ Necessity or Not ■

Returning to the original question, with what this Church has accomplished, perhaps the necessity has become a high level of relative necessity. Not absolute, but surely this Church cannot be ignored. American culture does not absolutely need the Roman Catholic Church, but now it seems hard to get along without it. Western culture may not have needed this Church, but in fact this Church has colored European civilization too deeply. For some to even begin to understand Europe means to acknowledge the Roman Church.

This work attempts to study the origins of Christianity and Roman Christianity and its meaning today. This may not add to the degree of necessity, but it fulfills the age-old call of faith seeking understanding. What the Church has been colors what the Church is now and what the Church will become. The origins are Jerusalem and Rome. The Church remains one, holy, catholic and apostolic and carries on a specific mission. The Church unites people into a community through word and sacrament. Through its service to the world and humanity, this one community offers the spiritual sacrifice of a life well lived in faith and joined to the one sacrifice of Jesus in worship.

Study Questions

1. Why should anyone speak of necessity with regard to the Church? Would it be better to speak of the need for religion?
2. Do you personally need the Church? If so, what kind of necessity do you feel?
3. What contribution has the Roman Catholic Church made to American culture?
4. How do you think Western culture would be different without the influence of the Church?
5. Are there differences between generations with regard to the necessity of the Church? If so, why?

Notes

1. The very use of "Catholic" immediately causes some hesitation. Most people think of the Catholic Church as being equivalent and limited to "Roman Catholic." In fact, the Catholic Church includes the Roman Church and some twenty-two other Churches that share the same faith and the same sacraments and are under the one bishop of Rome. This will be discussed further.

2. The current literature on the role of women in the Church would demand a separate volume. The issue will be discussed in Chapter 12.

3. Cf. Karl Rahner, *Revelation and Tradition* (New York: Herder and Herder, 1965), 9–25.

4. This particular study cannot be treated fully within this volume. Since it is an important pastoral concern, see Kenneth Himes and James Coriden, "Pastoral Care of the Divorced and Remarried," *Theological Studies,* Vol. 57(1996), 97–123.

2.

Roman Christianity

Trying to investigate historically and accurately what happened almost two thousand years ago causes problems. The sources are limited and the conclusions tentative. The study of the origins of Christianity in the city of Rome both tantalizes the scholar and disappoints. Many want clear and definite conclusions supporting present practice. Others, for whatever reasons, wish to avoid any conclusions. The study of early Christianity in Rome in this century has resulted in conclusions that satisfy few: less for those who want more and too much for those who want little.

Christianity probably arrived in Rome in the 40s.[1] In less than two decades after the death of Jesus, the Roman Christian community was alive and well. In the epistle to the Romans (written toward the end of the 50s), Paul remarks that he wanted to go to Rome for some time. Since Suetonius, the Roman historian, writes of Jews being expelled in 49 because of some controversy over "Chrestos," then surely Christianity was in Rome in the 40s. This alone should cause wonder. A rather obscure Jewish preacher who was crucified in Jerusalem is proclaimed messiah in Rome, the center of the then known world, within fifteen years after his death.

Since the Jews constantly made disturbances at the instigation of Chrestos, he [Claudius] expelled them from Rome *(Suetonius 25,4)*.

Tradition maintains that Rome was evangelized from Jerusalem. Most scholars will also accept the position that a number of these Jewish Christians in Rome were judaizers, those wanting to maintain some of the Jewish observances (moderate judaizer) and those who claimed that one first had to become a Jew before becoming a Christian (extreme judaizer). Also, since Paul writes to

11

the Christian community in Rome, mentioning many names (Rom 16:3–16), most conclude that just as Rome had many synagogues, so there were many, or at least several, house churches in Rome.

■ Paul's Letter to the Romans ■

The presence of encouraging words to the strong and speaking of the needs of the weak in chapter fourteen of Romans also insinuates that the Roman Christian community was divided. Inscriptions from the period show that they were united in the same language (Greek) and may have been predominantly Gentile but divided with regard to Jewish influences. Rome probably had several distinct groups in the middle part of the first century.

ROMAN GROUPS

1. Jews who maintained their commitment to Judaism and rejected Christ and Christianity.
2. Jewish Christians who accepted Christianity but maintained some Jewish observances.
3. Jewish Christians who accepted Christianity and demanded that Gentiles first become Jews.
4. Gentile Christians who had accepted some Jewish observance (moderately or in an extreme way).
5. Gentiles who accepted a law-free gospel.
6. Gentiles who remained pagan.

Thus, by a great variety of opinions, the Christian community at Rome was divided, and Paul seems to have been aware of all of this. Even the question of the collection in Romans 15 would have caused a mixed reaction. The Jewish Christians loyal to Jerusalem may have been reluctant to involve themselves with a collection coming from law-free gospel communities. The Gentile Christians in Rome may have been reluctant to contribute to a Jerusalem church to avoid the idea that they were vassals and dependent upon their particular understanding of the Jesus tradition.

During this period a strong nationalism existed among Jews. They would have been sensitive to anything that would violate Jewish distinctiveness and privileges. Thus, for some Jews, to preach that Gentiles could experience the same saving presence of God as Jews and without the law could easily cause conflict. This might explain the expulsion of Jews from Rome referred to by Suetonius. Those who advocated the acceptance of Gentiles without the observance of the law (followers of Paul) would have caused great tumult, especially since Christianity had not yet been separated from Judaism.

■ Paul and Rome ■

Undoubtedly, Paul's gospel was suspect in Rome. There also is no doubt that some of his converts were too liberal in their interpretation of the law-free gospel, as is evident in the problems in Corinth. His harsh words in Galatians probably reached Jerusalem and then might very well have reached the Christian communities in Rome as well. For all these reasons Paul personally, and the gospel he preached, would have appeared suspect in the Roman Christian community.

Paul needed the Roman Church to help him in the collection. He also needed the Roman Christians to use their influence with the Jerusalem church. As a Gentile and Jewish Christian community with strong roots in Jerusalem, they had a better chance of being heard than Paul. He needed to be accepted by both because he believed that the overriding necessity was the unity of the gospel and the unity of the Church. Paul did not want to advocate two separate churches and so was willing to compromise to bring about a sense of unity between the Jewish Christians and the Gentile Christians. He wanted to promote mutual tolerance and esteem within the community, and his letter and his journey were directed to that end. This also would give him a good base as he pushed on to Spain and continued to preach his gospel to the Gentiles.

Paul had changed his approach but not his fundamental teaching. In Galatians he preached a justification by faith apart from the law. In Romans he preached the righteousness of God revealed through faith apart from the law to Jews and then to Gentiles. His one gospel remains universal even if he admitted that for the sake of peace and unity, if some Jewish Christians wanted to observe some Jewish practices, that was acceptable, provided they were not imposed on Gentiles. For their part, the Gentiles should respect these historical Jewish roots and continue to have esteem for the fellow Christians of Jewish origin even if the latter chose to observe some Jewish practices. In this way Paul could encourage the strong but also maintain a support for the weak. Unity remained his chief concern.

From the epistle to the Romans[2] certain conclusions seem evident about this community in the middle of the first century.

1. Rome probably was a predominantly Gentile church but included Jewish as well as some Gentile Christians who advocated a strong commitment to the law.
2. All Christians in Rome needed to recognize that God offered universal salvation apart from the law to all people.
3. The gospel preached by Paul should be accepted by all Roman Christians. It was authentic and Paul was not ashamed of it.
4. The Roman Church had strong ties to Jerusalem. Paul needed the support of the Roman Church in his mission to Jerusalem.
5. Specific problems existed in the Roman Christian community: e.g., the observance or nonobservance of holidays and the question of eating meat and drinking wine.
6. The Roman Church needed mutual tolerance and esteem among the various members of the community. Paul saw his teaching responding to this need.

Above all Paul preached service to the one gospel that Christians acknowledged all over the empire. This one preaching invited Jew and Gentile alike to accept the gracious love of God offered to all apart from the law, through his Son Jesus the Christ (Rom 1:2–5).

■ Paul and Peter in Rome ■

Such was the situation of the Christian community when Paul arrived in Rome as a prisoner in the early 60s (Acts 28:14). No one can be sure when Peter arrived in Rome, but surely both apostles are identified with the city at this period and tradition maintains that they both were martyred in the mid-60s. Rome, which was the political, social, cultural and economic capital of the world, could also claim as part of its history the two best-known apostles of Christianity.

This twofold apostolic presence is mentioned toward the end of the century (C.E. 96) by Clement writing from Rome (5:3–5, C.E. 90–100) and Ignatius, a decade or two after, writing to Rome (1,1, C.E. 110). Although most scholars believe that Christianity preceded both Peter and Paul to Rome, Irenaeus, a century later, could write of Peter and Paul founding the Church at Rome (*Adv. Haer.* 3,3,3, C.E. 180–199). With such a distinguished pedigree, Rome would become the most important episcopal see within what would eventually become the Roman Catholic Church.[3]

To understand Christianity in Rome from the time of the epistle to the Romans to the letter of Clement (58–96), a study of

1 Peter, written from Rome between 80 and 90, and Hebrews, written to Christians in Rome sometime after 70, offers considerable help. Although any conclusion is only a hypothesis, these two letters give further insights into the Roman Christian community.[4]

The Church of God which sojourns in Rome to the Church of God which sojourns in Corinth...
                    —*Clement to the Church at Corinth 1,1*

Ignatius...to the Church that has found mercy in the greatness of the Most High Father and in Jesus Christ...to the Church also which holds the presidency in the place of the country of the Romans...
                    —*Ignatius of Antioch to the Romans 1,1*

Peter and Paul were evangelizing in Rome and laying the foundation of the Church.
                    —*Irenaeus, Adversus Haereses 3,1,1*

The blessed Apostles Peter and Paul having founded and built up the Church of Rome, they handed over the office of the episcopate to Linus.
                    —*Irenaeus, Adversus Haereses 3,3,3*

During this period, Christianity in Rome moved from a predominantly Gentile-influenced Christianity ultimately to an almost completely Gentile-influenced Christianity. Since Peter was frequently understood in the early tradition as one who was accepted in both Jewish Christian and Gentile Christian churches, this community at Rome came to be more associated with him.

The Paul of Romans modified his position from the Paul of Galatians. Eventually, through the writings of Luke in Acts, this more mellow Paul was joined to the tradition of Peter so that Clement could refer to both Peter and Paul as "pillars" of what will become the Roman Catholic Church.

■ 1 Clement[5] ■

Clement, writing around 96, refers to the "jealous zeal" among Christians that led to persecution and death. This might refer to the actual death of the "pillars" of the Church. Infighting would have been prevalent, with various factions within Christianity claiming true allegiance. In such a confused period, the eventual decision of Clement and others to follow the development of the hierarchical Church takes on more meaning.

A debated question among scholars concerns the identity of this Clement as well as his function. Was he a consul, or a member of the household of a consul? Was he a Jew who became a Christian or a Jew by background who was raised a Christian, or a Gentile who converted to Christianity or a Gentile raised as a Christian? Was he in fact the bishop of Rome or one among several leaders?[6]

SHEPHERD OF HERMAS

Therefore shall you write two little books and send one to Clement and one to Grapte. Clement shall then send it to the cities abroad, because that is his duty and Grapte shall instruct the widows and orphans. But you shall read it in this city along with the presbyters who are in charge of the Church.

2,4,3

Clement certainly wrote representing the Church of Rome. His letter is sent "from the Church of God which sojourns in Rome." *The Shepherd of Hermas* (also written in Rome around 100–125) refers to a Clement who had the responsibility of sending letters to other churches from Rome. Irenaeus wrote of Clement as having been allotted the bishopric of Rome in third place from the apostles. Linus and Anacletus had preceded him. While many may want to see Clement as functioning with full Petrine office in relationship to other churches—and thus the reason and right for letter writing—historical evidence shows that the monarchical episcopacy was not functioning in Rome until 140–150 C.E.[7] Clement may have been one of several presbyter bishops who functioned in Rome. The actual letter, 1 Clement, may have been sent by the collective Roman leadership and written by their secretary Clement, who was also a presbyter bishop.[8]

■ Leadership in Rome ■

Whether Rome had several presbyter bishops who eventually became one bishop remains an unsolved question. All signs, however, point to the plurality of presbyter bishops. What becomes evident is that the bishopric of Rome saw itself as heir to the pastoral care of Peter and Paul, the principal apostles of early Christianity. Ignatius mentions that the Roman Church taught others (Rom 3:1), and in the following chapter of his letter he states that Peter and Paul gave orders to the Romans. It seems that the Roman Church did not function as an authority center but rather as a pastoral center that would offer correction and admonishment among brethren that loved each other. Just as Paul wrote to admonish, so the see that related itself to Paul and Peter could write not to control but to admonish, expecting a favorable response.

With the destruction of Jerusalem in 70 and the dispersal of the Jerusalem church, the Church of Rome might be expected to assume responsibility to give guidance and direction to other churches, especially missionary churches. The movement from a more collegial church structure based on charisms to an institutional Church resulted from sociological and psychological reasons as well as theological reasons. Evidently the Church in Rome at the end of the first century assumed a leadership role in Christianity. The monarchical episcopacy, however, probably developed in other churches in Christianity before it took shape in Rome.[9]

Christianity at the end of the first century was besieged from within and without. Clement, and others like him, appealed to order, based on a clear structure of presbyter, bishop, deacon. This, joined to an understanding of levitical priesthood from Judaism, would give internal solidarity. Following the example of imperial Rome, Clement advocated obedience to ecclesiastic authorities in all matters of teaching and discipline. Christianity survived in human terms precisely because it offered a close-knit organization.

You must all follow the bishop as Jesus Christ follows the Father, and the presbytery as to the apostles. Reverence the deacons as you would the command of God. Let no one do anything of concern to the Church without the bishop. Let that be a valid Eucharist which is celebrated by the bishop or by one whom he appoints. Wherever the bishop appears let the people be there; just as wherever Christ is, there is the Catholic Church.

Ignatius to the Church of Smyrna 8,1

Subsequent events in the Church at Rome demonstrated the wisdom of Clement to follow a clear path calling for order in worship and obedience while still allowing diversity. The community of the gospel of John, which clearly had problems with any unbridled

Petrine authority, gave to Peter, and then, in all probability, to his successors, a pastoral charge provided that the holder of office loved Jesus and was willing to die for the flock (Jn 21:15–19). The community of the beloved disciple disintegrated with the death of its leader. The more organized and hierarchical community survived.

That Nero martyred both Peter and Paul in Rome also helped Rome to establish its position in Christianity. The true pastor as expressed in the gospel of John died for the flock in Rome. Paul himself remarked on the faith in Rome when he wrote his letter to the Romans (Rom 1:8), and he who suffered much met his death in Rome under Nero, joining the leader of the twelve. Ignatius of Antioch half a century later spoke of Rome as preeminent in love, nourished by the presence of Peter and Paul. The Roman Catholic Church today lives in the light of this legacy of faith and the love of Christ witnessed by Peter and Paul.

■ The Roman Church ■

The contemporary Roman Church then can trace its origins to Christianity in Rome shortly after the death of Jesus. This early Christian community was composed of both Jewish and Gentile Christians with some strong influence from the Jerusalem church. Very quickly the Roman Church became associated with Peter and Paul. Also, early in the development of Christianity this Roman Church assumed a specific role in relationship to other churches in the empire, especially after the destruction of Jerusalem in 70 and the dispersal of the Jerusalem church. Eventually, Rome followed the example of other Christian communities and structured itself after the model of the empire with one presbyter bishop in charge.

What Rome eventually became has roots in the earliest Jesus tradition but was also influenced by other factors. The very position of Rome as the center of the known world contributed to its preeminence in the Christian Church. The close association with Peter and Paul, the principal apostles of early Christianity, also contributed to its influence. Finally, sociological, psychological, anthropological, and theological needs for an organized and hierarchical Church all contributed to lay the foundations for the Roman Catholic Church as we know it today.

Study Questions

1. Christianity arrived in Rome early, probably in the 40s. Does this have any significance?

2. The origin of Roman Christianity probably came from a conservative Jewish Christian church in Jerusalem. Does this help to explain the Church at Rome in the earliest days?

3. Why was Paul so interested in Rome?

4. What do you like about the tradition of Peter and Paul at Rome? Do they still have significance for Christianity?

5. The great differences in the Church at Rome mirror the differences present throughout Christianity. What guidance can this offer to the Church today?

6. Paul's gospel was suspect in Rome. How does the law-free gospel remain within Christianity?

7. Clement and other presbyter/ bishops helped develop a hierarchical Church. Why was this necessary? What value does it offer?

8. The Church needs authority. Why?

9. What insights into the contemporary Church can be discovered in the origins of Christianity in Rome?

10. How does the Roman Church differ from the other Christian churches?

Notes

1. Many works may be consulted with regard to Christianity in Rome. See in particular R. Brown, *Priest and Bishop* (New York: Paulist, 1970); R. Brown and J. Meier, *Antioch and Rome* (New York: Paulist, 1982); D. W. O'Connor, *Peter in Rome* (New York: Columbia University, 1969). For a fuller bibliography see Brown, *Antioch...*

2. Cf. John F. O'Grady, *Pillars of Paul's Gospel: Galatians and Romans* (New York: Paulist, 1992), 83–88.

3. K. Lake, *The Apostolic Fathers,* Loeb Classical Library (New York, 1930), has both the original text of the writings of the early fathers as well as an English translation. Another anthology of many early texts can be found in W. Jurgens, *The Faith of the Early Fathers* (Collegeville: Liturgical Press, 1970).

4. Cf. Brown, *Antioch...,* 92–159.

5. Ibid., 159–183.

6. Ibid., 161–162.

7. Ibid., 163. "Indeed, the signal failure of Ignatius (c. 110) to mention the single-bishop in his letter to the Romans (a very prominent theme in his other letters), and the usage of *Hermas*, which speaks of plural presbyters (*Vis.* 2.4.2) and bishops (*Sim.* 9.27.2), make it likely that the single-bishop structure did not come to Rome until c. 140–150."

8. Ibid., 164.

9. Ibid., 77. "...the presiding teacher-prophet at Antioch became the one bishop, the other teachers and prophets became the college of elders, and the other church workers became the deacons. Writing between A.D. 108–117, Ignatius can take this structure for granted in his own church as he attempts to shore up the position of the bishop in the churches in Asia Minor."

■ PART II ■

The Bible and the Church

*T*oo often Christians think that the Church's belief in Jesus has little to do with the Old Testament. Some see the New Testament as the fulfillment of the Old Testament and leave it at that. However, Jesus and the Church can never exist apart from the Old Testament with its traditions and theology. The understanding of Jesus, Christianity and the Church depends on both a love and an appreciation of the history and traditions of Israel.

Having called the Jewish people into a covenantal relationship, God never has reneged on this responsibility. The creator of all called a people to be priestly, to be the one chosen people elected to be a sign of God's salvation to all nations. This people offered to God the worship of the heart and never were supposed to separate their election from the call to take care of those in need.

The history of Israel demonstrates human failure. Jesus alone lived as a sign of God's saving presence to all. He was the only true priest. He offered the spiritual sacrifice of a life lived for others as he cared for anyone in need. His meaning finds its roots in the ancient covenant between God and the Jewish people.

The Church continues this ministry of Jesus by sharing in his priesthood and living as the sign of God's saving presence throughout the ages. The members of the Church join their spiritual offering to that of Jesus himself by taking care of those in need.

Only Jesus truly fulfills the human election recorded in the Old Testament traditions. Only Jesus continues to function as the perfect priest in the Church through his Spirit. Only Jesus brings

21

salvation and redemption. The Church fulfills its mission only because Jesus lives on in the Church through the presence of the Holy Spirit.

The Church looks to the Bible for its self-understanding and finds in the Bible its meaning and origin. All of the Bible reflects the word of God and all of the Bible belongs to the Church. Knowing the traditions helps in understanding how the Church should function today.

3.

Election and Covenant in the Biblical Foundations for the Church

*H*uman destiny finds fulfillment in God. Every person has been chosen to share in the glory of God through creation. All peoples of all times have their origin in God and find their fulfillment in God:

> Let us make man in our image after our likeness... So God created man in his own image; in the image of God he created him, male and female he created them. (Gen 1:26–27)

While all people are created in the image of God, historically the Israelites were chosen for election. Among all the nations of the world the small group of people called Israelites, or Jews, became God's special people. Ezekiel reminds his listeners of their origins:

> Thus says the Lord God to Jerusalem: By origin you are of the land of Canaan; your father was an Amorite and your mother a Hittite. As for your birth, the day you were born your navel cord was not cut; you were neither washed with water nor anointed, nor were you rubbed with salt, not swathed in swaddling clothes. No one looked on you with pity or compassion to do any of these things for you. Rather, you were thrown out on the ground as something loathsome, the day you were born.
>
> Then I passed by and saw you weltering in your blood. I said to you: "Live in your blood and grow like a plant in the field." You grew and developed, you came to the age of puberty; your breasts were formed, your hair had grown, but you were still stark naked. Again I

passed by you and saw that you were old enough for love. So I spread the corner of my cloak over you to cover your nakedness. I swore an oath to you and entered into a covenant with you; you became mine, says the Lord God.

Then I bathed you with water, washed away your blood and anointed you with oil. I clothed you with an embroidered gown, put sandals of fine leather on your feet; I gave you a fine linen sash and silk robes to wear. I adorned you with jewelry; I put bracelets on your arms, a necklace about your neck, a ring in your nose, pendants in your ears, and a glorious diadem upon your head. Thus you were adorned with gold and silver; your garments were of fine linen, silk and embroidered cloth. Fine flour, honey and oil were your food. You were exceedingly beautiful, with the dignity of a queen. You were renowned among the nations for your beauty, perfect as it was, because of my splendor which I had bestowed on you, says the Lord God. (Ez 16:3-14)

Israel could lay no claim on God for election.[1] Among all the nations of the world, Israel was chosen to be God's people. Israel was blessed beyond measure and given God's own Word as its own. The meaning of election, however, was not an election to leisure and self-importance. God chose Israel for a specific role in history in relationship to other peoples. [2] All people are destined to share in the plan of God, but it was Israel alone that knew this plan. God had revealed and God wished Israel to respond.

■ Sign of Salvation to the Nations ■

The chosen people would manifest God to the nations. Israel as God's people existed in history as a sign of salvation to the nations.[3] Other nations and cultures were meant to recognize in Israel the presence of the one true God. They were to stream into the city of Jerusalem to learn of this God and with worship, share in the saving presence of God in human history.

The priest makes the divine manifest in human history. The priest joins heaven to earth and earth to heaven. The priest mediates between divinity and humanity. The books of Exodus and Deuteronomy[4] offer the foundation for the priesthood of all believers in Israel. Israel alone knows the one true God, and as God's chosen people they will reveal this God to others.

> Now therefore if you obey my voice and keep my covenant, you shall be my own possession among all the peoples; for all the earth is mine and you shall be to me a kingdom of priests and a holy nation. (Ex 19:5–6)[5]

> ...but you who cling to the Lord your God, are all alive today. Therefore I teach you the statutes and decrees as the Lord my God has commanded me, that you may observe them in the land you are entering to occupy. Observe them carefully; thus will you give evidence of your wisdom and intelligence to the nations, who will hear all of these statutes and say: "This great nation is truly and wise and intelligent people." (Dt 4:4–6)

> For you are a people sacred to the Lord, your God who has chosen you from all the nations on the face of the earth to be a people peculiarly his own. (Dt 14:2)

> He will then raise you high in praise and renown and glory above all other nations he has made, and you will be a people sacred to the Lord your God as he promised. (Dt. 26:19)

■ True Worship ■

Unlike other nations, which engaged in often bizarre sacrifices, including human sacrifice, Israel offered the only true worship, the worship of the heart. God did not want holocausts but the offering of a "humble and contrite heart."

> For you are not pleased with sacrifices;
> should I offer a holocaust, you would not accept it.
> My sacrifice, O God, is a contrite spirit;
> a heart contrite and humbled, O God, you will not
> spurn. (Ps 51:18–19)

Sacrifices of bulls and grain offerings please only if they express in ritual form the offering of a life lived for God and for God's people. Without this heart of the sacrifice, all such offerings become ritual lies, an abomination to the Lord.

■ Care for the Poor ■

Israel also had an obligation to care for the poor, the forgotten, the abandoned, those who had no one else on whom they could trust and rely. The unfortunate of the earth would become the special care of God's people. The poor and all who help the poor would live together with complete dependence on the power and goodness of God. As Israel was once abandoned and in need of freedom and liberation and justice in Egypt, so Israel must always remember the history and condition of old, and care for the needs of others.

> The needy will never be lacking in the land; that is why I command you to open your hand to your poor and needy kinsmen in your country. (Dt 15:11)

God would bless Israel if Israel took care of those in need (Dt 15:1–11). A nation that had benefited from the goodness and benevolence of God should always carefully look after the less fortunate. Such practices please God and ensure continued blessings.

If Israel fulfilled this role, it would flourish as a holy nation, and other peoples would come to the holy city of Jerusalem and offer to Israel the dignity and honor due to the nation that revealed the mystery of God's plan for all creation.

> Nations shall walk by your light and kings by your radiance. Raise your eyes and look about; they all gather and come to you, your sons come from afar and your daughters in the arms of their nurses. (Is 60:3–4)

■ Failure in Election ■

The Old Testament, however, records the failure of God's people to fulfil their destiny. The continuation of the quotation from Ezekiel accuses Israel:

> But you trusted in your beauty, and played the harlot because of your renown and lavished your harlotries on any passer-by...You also played the harlot with the Egyptians...you played the harlot with the Assyrians...also with the trading land of Chaldea. (Ez 16:15, 26–29)

God called his people to be a sign of salvation to the nations, but that people accepted the gods of the nations and made them its own, even offering human sacrifice (Ez 16:20–21). In ancient times, to accept the sovereignty of another nation included accepting the gods and religious practices of that nation. When Israel entered into treaties with its powerful neighbors, Egypt, Assyria, and Chaldea, Israel forgot the covenant.

Israel desecrated true worship with the introduction of false gods:

> Then I said to them: Throw away each of you the detestable things that have held your eyes; do not defile yourself with the idols of Egypt; I am the Lord your God. But they rebelled against me and refused to listen to me. (Ez 20:7)

The failure of Israel included its treatment of the poor and needy. The prophets continually judged the sins of Israel and recorded the oppression of those who were needy:

> Thus says the Lord: For three crimes of Israel and for four, I will not revoke my word, because they sell the just man for silver and the poor man for a pair of sandals. They trample the heads of the weak into the dust of the earth, and force the lowly out of the way. Son and father go to the same prostitute profaning my holy name. (Am 2:6–7)

■ The Covenant[6] ■

Election in Israel includes an understanding of the Hebrew relationship to God expressed by the word *berith*.[7] Most translations use the English word "covenant." Although that is the usual translation, it evokes the image of a bilateral treaty, and this fails to express the nuance of the Hebrew. Some translate *berith* as obligation or responsibility. Even here confusion arises, since most people conclude that in a covenant with God the responsibility lies with the

---

COVENANT

Covenant of Abraham: Gen 15:18
Covenant of Moses:
   Sinai: Ex 19:1–8
   Horeb: Ex 33:6–23;
Covenant of Joshua: Jos 24:16–25
Covenant of David: 2 Sam 23:5

recipient of the covenant, with people, and not with God. In the Old Testament tradition the responsibility lies rather with God. Once God has spoken, God will never go back on what was said.[8] God remains faithful.

When scholars treat covenant in the Old Testament, many are quick to point out that Sinai was a conditional covenant and the Davidic covenant is unconditional.[9] Certainly the language used in the writings of the Old Testament encourage such distinctions. In a more careful study of even Sinai, however, God always relents despite the presence of terrible evil and sin. God will not abandon Israel, the people he called so long ago.

As a chosen and special group, God wished Israel to live as a chosen people and fulfill the functions of the covenant by being a sign of salvation to the nations, offering true worship and caring for the poor. When Israel joyfully fulfilled its calling, Israel became a nation of priests for the sake of others, bringing all to recognize the one true God:

> Now therefore if you will obey my voice and keep my covenant you shall be my own possession among all the peoples; for all the earth is mine, and you shall be to me a kingdom of priests and a holy nation. (Ex 19:5–6)

The holy nation and the kingdom of priests applied to all Israelites, to all Jews. Their destiny involved not only a special relationship to God but a responsibility to all other peoples. Priests act in the name of people in the presence of God. They act in God's name, making people aware of the saving presence of God in all of human life. Such was the call of Israel.

To support the chosen people, God expressed certain qualities toward Israel. Covenantal virtues characterized all of the dealings of God with the chosen nation. The *hesed*[10] and *emeth*[11] of God bound together both participants in the covenant. As a result, the Old Testament overflows with references to these two covenantal virtues.

> The Lord has made his salvation known;
> in the sight of the nations he has revealed his justice.
> He has remembered his kindness and
> his faithfulness toward the house of Israel.
> All the ends of the earth have seen
> the salvation by our God. (Ps 98:2–3)

■ *Hesed* ■

The Hebrew word *hesed* cannot be adequately translated into English. Sometimes translators will use the word "compassion," other times "kindness" and still other times "mercy." Each English word conveys some insight into the wealth of meaning contained in this small Hebrew word.

The God of Israel is a compassionate God. The compassionate person enters into the experience of the other, and if the experience is good, the moment is doubly enjoyed. If the experience is bad or painful, the sorrow is more easily borne through the presence of the compassionate person. God was compassionate with Israel, entering into its joys and sadness, celebrating and helping to bear the sorrow.

The God of Israel treated the chosen people with kindness. The kind person emphasizes the positive, seeking the good and always overlooking the evil. God always saw the good in the people of Israel, and even when Israel was punished, eventually the kind God turned to forgiveness.

Everyone has failed, sinned, missed the mark. The God of Israel knew the sins and failures of Israel and always forgave. God held no grudges. Although punishing Israel for a time, God always relented and restored the people, promising eventually an eternal restoration and fulfillment.

■ *Emeth* ■

Emeth likewise causes problems for the translators. Sometimes the word in English becomes "truth," or "fidelity," or "something perduring or enduring." "Fidelity" seems the best translation. God remains faithful to the chosen people no matter what. The fidelity of God outlasts all human fidelity and puts to shame any human attempt to remain faithful in the midst of betrayal and rejection.

God always remains faithful in the midst of human infidelity, for God remains God. Humans might react differently in the midst of infidelity, but God must continue as the faithful one; otherwise human failure controls God. Divinity demands fidelity. Once God has spoken, the word remains. The history of Israel is the history of failure on the part of the chosen people and the eternal, perduring, enduring, compassion, kindness and forgiveness of God.

■ The Glory of God[12] ■

In the history of Israel the glory of God figures prominently. *Kabod* etymologically signifies "weight" or "heaviness" and can be applied to both people and God. When applied to God in the Old Testament, the issue becomes rather complex with a mixture of sophisticated theology and concrete manifestations.

The most primitive form of glory in the Pentateuch involved light and the pillar of cloud. Both fire and the cloud were concrete manifestations in the Exodus tradition of the presence and protection of God. When the Israelites saw the cloud (Ex 16:10; 24:16–18; Lev 9:6, 23) or the pillar of fire, they knew that God was near and they felt secure. Later in the prophets the glory of God is a canopy over Israel and a protection (Is 4:5; 58:8; Mi 1:15).

Frequently the glory is associated with light. Thus, the earth as full of the glory of God refers to the light that creation contains and manifests. The presence of light in contrast to the darkness, also present in creation, reminds the Israelites of the presence and protection of its God.

In later books glory loses some of its concrete meaning, and to see the glory of God means to see and experience the saving deeds of God (Is 35:2; 40:5; 59:19; 66:18–19; Ps 63:2). The glory of God manifests who God is, and this becomes evident in what God has done for the people. God is glorified when the goodness and power of God become manifest. Historically the exodus experience manifests in a paramount way the glory of God. God's power overcomes the power of the pharaoh; God's goodness takes a captive people and gives them freedom and a land. The divinity of their God becomes manifest in the exodus experience and then in the experience of Sinai. To give glory to God means to recognize the divinity of God and in particular to see God's saving presence. God is good and God is powerful. God protects and hovers over Israel like a canopy. God will assist Israel because of his glory (Ps 79:9). Since divinity, the power and goodness of God, endures forever, Israel can be confident that the protecting God will shelter it forever. Israel is created by the glory of God in the exodus and for the glory of God (Is 43:7). In this sense the psalmist prays that all peoples will see the glory of God. "The heavens proclaim his justice and all peoples see his glory" (Ps 97:6).

The ancient peoples did not have abstract notions of divinity. Divinity meant something practical and concrete. The divinity of God connoted God's power and goodness. This understanding becomes evident in *hesed* and *emeth*—qualities attributed to God in the Old Testament. God wills to save. The saving presence of God permeates the history of Israel and God always remains kind and compassionate. God remains faithful, always sees the goodness in the chosen people and is always forgiving. The goodness of the heart of God gives rise to compassion and kindness and mercy. Through the experience of these divine virtues, people come to recognize God's glory and the very nature of God.

■ *Kahal* of God[13] ■

The word *kahal* signifies the religious assembly of the Israelites precisely as God's holy and priestly people. When the Israelites gathered in worship they acknowledged their indebtedness to God and pledged their willingness to live according to the covenant with its functions and its virtues. They would be God's holy and priestly people by living in a way that would draw other nations to Jerusalem and their God. They would offer the only acceptable sacrifice and they would care for the poor. When they also both experienced and manifested the *hesed* and *emeth* of God, they recognized God's presence and gave glory to God.

Historically and theologically no one can separate the covenant from God's glory and the functions and virtues of the covenant. Each one interacts and fulfills the other. The assembled congregation of God's people have lived the covenantal virtues. They have taken care of the poor. In so doing they offer the one true sacrifice of the life well lived and become a beacon, a sign of salvation, for the nations. They recognize the glory of God in the protecting and saving presence of God, and in their living and assembling in worship they give glory to God. Israel fulfilled its destiny as a priestly nation when they lived their covenant with God. The people of Israel remained God's holy and priestly people. They did not always live as this holy people, but they never lost their calling to offer the sign of God's saving presence to all nations, to offer the sacrifice of the heart and to care for the poor. They lived in history as the assembly of God's chosen ones.

■ Hierarchical Priesthood in Israel[14] ■

In the history of Israel a hierarchical priesthood also functioned. The origins of these offices and duties, however, lie shrouded in darkness. In the patriarchal period the people worshiped at local shrines, and in most cases the head of the household functioned as

---

HIERARCHICAL PRIESTHOOD

The Jewish priesthood of Levites and the Zadokites developed as a professional class based more on lineage than on office or vocation. The early priestly function consisted mainly of the consulting of the lots to determine the will of God. Gradually priesthood shifted more to worship with cultic sacrifice. The obscure figure of Melchizedek represents the priest-king, independent of the levitical line. This later influenced Christian priesthood.

---

priest. Through a careful analysis of the Pentateuch, scholars have recognized that the priesthood as an office developed over a period of years even though the editors of the Pentateuch situated it in the desert as fully developed.

This hierarchical priesthood emphasizes the sanctification of the priest by his role which consisted of giving oracles, the leading of ritual and the teaching of the law. After the exile, the priests took on more kingly roles with a gradual confusion of power. With the birth of the synagogue, during and after the Babylonian exile, the role of the word of God took on greater importance. In New Testament times the role of the priest was more tied in with politics, power and prestige. Often the role of the people as priestly became forgotten in the developing hierarchical priesthood of Israel. Jesus would recall the earlier traditions.

■ Jesus: Election, Covenant and Priesthood ■

Like the ancient Jewish people, God chose Jesus and elected him as the favored one. Jesus fully incarnated the covenant in his very being. As the Christ, the anointed one of God, he remains for Christians the perfect and only priest, not in the sense of the hierarchical priesthood but in the context of the priesthood of the people of Israel. He alone glorified God; he alone sanctified people. Jesus manifested the covenantal virtues. He lived and died as the sign of salvation for all. Jesus offered the true worship of a good life and cared for those in need.

The gospels do not present Jesus as priest in the usual sense of the word or in the context of the hierarchical priesthood. The gospel of John, however, presents in chapter 17 what can be considered a foundation of the priesthood of Jesus. In this chapter the evangelist presents Jesus as accomplishing his mission on earth. He has glorified God his Father by revealing his name:

I have given you glory on earth by finishing the work you gave me to do. Do you now, Father, give me glory at your side, a glory I had with you before the world began. I made your name known to those you gave me out of the world. These men you gave me were yours; they have kept your word. (Jn 17:4–6)

He made himself the holy one of God so that others may share in that same holiness. A key verse in the gospel of John expresses this meaning in the life and ministry of Jesus:

I make myself holy for their sakes now, that they may be holy in truth. (Jn 17:19)

Jesus gives glory to the Father through the sanctification of people. This is the fundamental element in the meaning of his priesthood. The glory of God becomes evident in Jesus when it becomes known through Jesus who God is: people recognize God as merciful and faithful. Throughout the Old Testament, God was present to the chosen people, and he always shows them the covenantal virtues. Jesus does likewise.

In the New Testament, Jesus alone is the glory of God (Heb 1:3). The fourth gospel joins in the prologue the glory of God with the qualities of mercy and fidelity, *hesed* and *emeth:*

...and we have seen his glory, the glory of.an only Son coming from the Father, filled with grace *(charis, hesed)* and truth *(alaetheias, emeth).* (Jn 1:14)

Jesus gives glory to the Father by revealing the name of God, by showing the divine qualities; Jesus has sanctified himself to show this glory and sanctifies others to grant them the same possibility of showing the glory of God by reflecting in their lives the qualities of God: mercy and fidelity. People may look upon Jesus and discover in him and in his life the same qualities associated with God and the chosen people in the Old Testament. Continuity and fulfillment bind together Jesus and the Old Testament covenant along with the priesthood of Israel.

■ Hebrews[15] ■

The author of Hebrews labors to present the priesthood of Jesus both in relationship to Jewish hierarchical priesthood and as superior to this priesthood. The epistle is divided into five sections. The author moves from the analysis of the position of Jesus in regard to God and people to an exhortation to the Christian people to live a life in accord with their sharing in the life of their high priest.

The first section (1–2) situates Jesus in relation to God and in the context of the angels. The author carefully presents the basic image of Jesus as Son of God (distinct from the angels) and brother to all humanity (like us as one of our race). This is the starting point for all future developments.

The second section (3–4) emphasizes the reality of the high priest. Believers have in Jesus one who obtains peace for them. The author presents the mercy of God in Jesus as well as emphasizes the solidarity of Jesus with people. He is named by God but is one taken from among people.

The third section (5–10) presents the more complete theme of Jesus as priest, using the vocabulary characteristic of the institution of Israelitic hierarchical priesthood: the offering of sacrifice, the purification of the people by blood, the entrance into the holy of holies and, in all of this, the superiority of the priesthood of Christ over the ancient hierarchical priesthood.

The fourth section (11:1–12:13) presents ideas on faith as the characteristic response to the reality of the priesthood of Christ. The author relates this faith today to the faith in the Old Testament. The presence of faith in Christ brings about a change in the mode of the faith expressed in the Old Testament.

The final section (12:14–13:18) exhorts the Christian people to join together charity and sanctity into a single reality, the authentic Christian life. The author moves from situating Christ in relationship to Israel, to the presentation of the true priesthood of Jesus, to the final exhortation to live a Christian life based on the same.

> ...therefore he had to become like his brethren in every way, that he might be a merciful and faithful high priest before God on their behalf, to expiate the sins of the people. Since he was himself tested through what he suffered, he is able to help those who are tempted. (Heb 2:17–18)[16]

Jesus as the high priest stands in sharp contrast to that office in Israel. Christ has not obtained social status or monetary remuneration or political power or even elevation among the people by his priesthood. Christ lived as high priest through the renunciation of privilege. Nor did he extol himself above the people: "He was assimilated to all," even to the extreme point of death. He became priest by offering himself in his ministry and in his death. Then, he gave full glory to his God.

In this passage the same two qualities, from the Old Testament as well as in the gospel of John, stand out: mercy and fidelity. These interpersonal qualities and virtues pertain to the relationship between God and the chosen people. Here they also express the mediation that Christ fulfills between God and the followers of Jesus.

■ Mercy ■

Jesus shows human mercy and compassion toward his followers as priest. To exhibit such virtues demands a prior experience of sadness, tribulation and joy. Christ had to sustain human suffering to have this relationship of compassion and mercy. This involved active service and a consoling ministry to those in need. The gospels record such a life and ministry. Jesus lived as a kind and compassionate Lord, particularly as portrayed in chapter 15 of Luke. Jesus the merciful prophet fulfilled all of the expectancy of the Old Testament in Matthew. He is the Son of Man unto death who brings the experience of mercy to those who call on him in faith in Mark. Jesus joins himself to his followers and, united to them, he loves them to the end in the gospel of John.

■ Faithfulness ■

Faithfulness belongs primarily to God who keeps faith. The covenant faith characterizes the attitude of God toward people. No matter what anyone may choose to do, the word of God remains faithful. God will never abandon people. God is the one who offers the firm foundation with powerful security to all who trust in what God has promised.

Christ as priest exemplifies the same quality. He lives and dies worthy of faith. God responded by enthroning Jesus and proclaiming him as Son. Jesus the high priest becomes perfected in the stability of his fidelity. He is worthy of trust as priest, and through him all can be certain to have sure access to the one loving God.

Sirach 6:6–16 observes that real fidelity is seen in tribulation. Because Jesus bore upon himself all tribulations and took on an ignominious death, his fidelity became apparent. This further emphasized the relationship of his fidelity to his followers. He is faithful in the midst of tribulations, and in the presence of tribulations not only does he not abandon his love and obedience to his God, but he also remains faithful to his commitment to people.

The conjunction of mercy and fidelity relates the priesthood of Christ to the covenantal virtues of God. In him all converge. Mercy *(hesed)* and divine fidelity *(emeth)* toward people characterized the life and death of Jesus. The same living and dying manifested human mercy and fidelity in relationship to God. The covenantal virtues become visible in human life, coming to people and shared in by all peoples in the return response to God. Moreover, these same virtues are manifested outward from Christ to include all of humankind. Jesus is the perfect mediator and perfect priest.

Hebrews continues commenting on the purpose of this high priesthood: the expiation of sins. Jesus lived and dies the faithful and merciful high priest who cleanses from sin; he makes people holy through ministry and death. The Son of the Father and brother of all professes the covenantal virtues and thus expiates for sins and makes people holy.

■ Hebrews and John 17 ■

The priesthood of Jesus in Hebrews concurs with the meaning of the gospel of John. Jesus glorified the Father when he used the power bestowed on him to give life to believers. This he accomplished by revealing the name of God. He has shown his disciples that God is Father and is merciful and faithful. Now the final moment of glorification has come for Jesus and his followers. God's glory, God's name, and divine qualities will be revealed in the Passover meal and in the offering of Jesus in dying and finally will culminate in the great sign of the glorification of Jesus: his death and resurrection.

In chapter 17 of John the author refers to the holiness of God: "Holy Father" (17:11), "Righteous Father" (17:25), and the holiness of Jesus: "I make myself holy" (17:19). The holiness, the nearness to God of those who have come to hear and to believe in the name of God, follows: "That they may be consecrated holy in truth" (17:19). The believers are made holy in "truth," in Jesus, and are sent to make the name of God known in this world, a proclamation that will manifest the glory of God. Jesus himself is the "truth" of God which makes people holy. This truth, known and preached, makes God present in the world as merciful and faithful and causes people to react to the nearness of God.

Everything present in these chapters can be related to the priesthood of all believers in Israel. Those who believe in Jesus are the sign to others that God is near and offers salvation. Believers in Jesus make God's name known to the nations. The followers of Jesus offer the true worship; they offer their holy lives as the sacrifice to God and render glory to God. Finally, they care for those who are in need. All of this Jesus had done as priest and now his followers will continue his ministry. Insofar as Jesus manifested the qualities of God and sanctified himself and others, he was a priest who completely fulfilled the calling of the priesthood of believers in the Old Testament. Now when believers manifest these same qualities, they fulfill their priestly function and render glory to God with Jesus.

■ The Church and the Priesthood of Israel and of Jesus ■

The later writings of the New Testament continue this same tradition from the Old Testament. The early Church proclaimed that Jesus was the savior for all, both Jew and Gentile, and that all nations will offer the worship of the heart. Spiritual sacrifice will characterize the call of believers to Christianity, and they will care for those in need.[17]

> Come to him, a living stone rejected by many but approved, nonetheless, and precious in God's edifice of spirit. Enter into a holy priesthood, offering spiritual sacrifices acceptable to God. You however are a chosen race, a royal priesthood, a holy nation, a people he claims for his own to proclaim the glorious works of the one who called you from darkness into his marvelous light. Once you were no people but now you are God's people; once there was no mercy for you but now you have found mercy. (1 Pet 2:4–6, 9–10)

In this short passage from 1 Peter, the author writes of the fulfillment and continuity of the destiny of Israel in Christianity. The spiritual sacrifice is a life well lived. The royal priesthood ties Christians to the task of manifesting salvation to the nations. In this same chapter, the author encourages good works to give glory to God.

After more than three thousand years this spiritual calling remains the same today. God enters into a covenant with people, calling them to accept election and the responsibility to live so that all may experience the saving presence of God. God still asks the worship of the heart and expects people to take care of each other.

These more than three thousand years of history have also seen the failure of both Jews and Christians to live up to the calling.

But God has not changed. The covenant remains the same. God shows mercy and fidelity to all even if people do not always respond. To understand the Christian Church demands an understanding of the history of Israel and its covenant. The foundation for the Church lies in the continuity between Israel, Jesus, and his followers in the Church. And the only one who lived and died according to the loving will of God still remains Jesus, the Jew.

Study Questions

1. What does election mean to you? Is human destiny involved?
2. If all are created in the image of God, does this mean that all people are equal? Yes or no? How or how not?
3. God chooses whomever he wants. Does this make God unfair?
4. The threefold call—to be a sign of salvation, to offer the true worship and to care for the poor—continues in Christianity. What does this all mean to you?
5. All of us fail in election and in responsibility. What difference does this make in our relationship to God?
6. What does covenant mean to you? Has your idea changed in the study of covenant in the Bible?
7. Why are the covenantal virtues so important in life?
8. The glory of God is the manifestation of power and goodness. Do people manifest the glory of God?
9. The hierarchical priesthood of Israel was present but not always so important. What does this offer to the understanding of the hierarchical priesthood in Christianity?
10. Jesus alone fulfilled the priesthood of Israel. What does this mean to Christianity?
11. Compare Hebrews and the gospel of John with regard to holiness and priesthood.

Notes

1. Cf. Dale Patrick, "Election," *The Anchor Bible Dictionary* (New York: Doubleday, 1992), 434–441; Patrick Miller, *Deuteronomy* (Louisville: John Knox, 1990), 110–114.

2. Miller notes: "The priesthood [in Israel] performed such a

role within Israel, so by analogy Israel as a priesthood would perform this role for the nations" (438).

3. Cf. G. von Rad, *Studies in Deuteronomy* (London, SCM, 1953), chapter 1.

4. "Whether or not the author of Deuteronomy was the first to speak of YHWH's choice of the people of Israel, this work contains the most thorough and penetrating reflection on the concept of election within Scripture." Patrick, "Election," 436.

5. "The use of the term 'priests' in the one phrase may allude to a role of mediation between God and the nations." Patrick, "Election," 438.

6. For a better understanding of covenant in general and the various types of covenants, see L. Boadt, *Reading the Old Testament* (New York: Paulist, 1984), 173–184. For a fuller understanding see Dennis McCarthy, *Treaty and Covenant* (Rome: Biblical Institute, 1963); George Mendenhall, "Covenant," 1179–1202.

7. The most extensive etymological and theological analysis of *berith* can be found in M. Weinfeld, *"berith," Theological Dictionary of the Old Testament* (Grand Rapids: Eerdmans, 1975), 253–279. *"Berith* implies first and foremost the notion of 'imposition,' 'liability,' or 'obligation'" (255).

8. Cf. George Mendenhall, "Covenant," *The Anchor Bible Dictionary*, Vol. 1, 1188.

9. Ibid., 1183, 118–119. Also cf. 1188.

10. Cf. H. J. Zobel, *"hesed," Theological Dictionary of the Old Testament* (Grand Rapids: Eerdmans, 1986), 44–64: " [*hesed*]…is used to express the permanence and constancy of Yahweh's kindness, its inviolability and trustworthiness" (p. 63).

11. *Emeth* is usually treated along with *hesed*. Certainly the study of the latter is more important than the former. The combination of both words can be found throughout the Old Testament.

12. Any standard dictionary of the Old Testament of the Bible will give further information on glory. Cf. G. H. Davies, "Glory," *Interpreters Dictionary of the Bible* (New York: Abingdon, 1962), 401–403.

13. Cf. P. S. Minear, "Church, Idea of," *Interpreters Dictionary,* 608–617.

14. Cf. W. Eichrodt, *Theology of the Old Testament* (London: SCM, 1961), 392–435.

15. Cf. R. Collins, *Letters That Paul Did Not Write* (Wilmington: Glazier, 1988), for a general overview of Hebrews. For a fuller

exegesis, see H. Attridge, *The Epistle to the Hebrews* (Philadelphia: Fortress, 1989).

16. Cf. Attridge, especially 94–103.

17. The Second Vatican Council specifically refers to the Church as the sign of salvation to the nations, *Lumen Gentium* 1, 9, 48. The *Catechism* also refers to the Church as the sign of salvation, sections 774, 775, 776. The council also emphasized the renewal of the liturgy as the expression of the true sacrifice of the heart and proclaimed a special concern for the poor.

4.

The Origins of the Church in the New Testament

T he Church in the New Testament continues the ministry of Jesus. Jesus himself fulfilled the Old Testament election of God's holy and priestly people, and he himself manifested the qualities of God associated with the covenant. This great tradition moves easily and quickly into the early communities. They took time to develop a hierarchical and institutional Church, but all the foundations for such a Church can be found in the witness of the various writings of the New Testament.[1] The diversity during this early period, however, becomes evident in any reading of the New Testament. The beginnings involve enthusiastic preachers who called people to repent, believe and be baptized (Acts 2:37–38).

■ Primitive Preaching ■

The earliest preaching[2] about Jesus, found in the summary statements of Acts, gives evidence that the early followers and preachers proclaimed that God has raised up the crucified Jesus. This Jesus had fulfilled his ministry of doing good, had sent the Holy Spirit, had fulfilled the Old Testament hopes and promises, and would come to judge the living and the dead. From this preaching arose the Christian Church. The emphasis lay on the power of the Spirit. God inspired the earliest followers of Jesus to reach out and proclaim the saving presence of God in the death and resurrection of Jesus. They became "enthusiastic" about the gospel and all that it might entail for humanity.

41

PRIMITIVE PREACHING

Fulfills Old Testament
Ministry of doing good
Crucified and risen
Sent Holy Spirit
Will come again

Response: Repent, believe, be baptized

■ Enthusiasm[3] ■

Christianity truly began as an enthusiastic movement. People had experienced the powerful presence of the Holy Spirit as recorded in the Acts of the Apostles and began a movement that eventually spread throughout the known world, from Jerusalem to Rome:

> He charged them not to depart from Jerusalem...
> "Before many days you will be baptized by the Holy
> Spirit." (Acts 1:4–5)

> And he [Paul] lived there [Rome] two whole years at his
> own expense and welcomed all who came to him,
> preaching the kingdom of God and teaching about the
> Lord Jesus Christ quite openly and unhindered (Acts
> 28:30).

The Acts of the Apostles, the record of early Christianity, begins in Jerusalem and ends in Rome. The movement of Christianity from a small geographical area in Asia Minor to Rome, the center of the world depended on enthusiasm and the power of the Spirit.

Paul himself was a preacher gifted with enthusiasm. He recognized the need for a spontaneous and exuberant preaching of Jesus. That enthusiasm would establish the Christian community while time and experience would bring the ordering of the enthusiasm into a developed Church.

In 1 Corinthians Paul recognized the presence of many ministries and responsibilities in this early community. Each had its charism which would be used for the edification of the community.

> Let all things be done for edification. If any speak in a
> tongue, let there be only two or at the most three, and each

in turn; and let one interpret. But if there is no one to interpret, let each of them keep silence in church and speak to himself and to God. Let two or three prophets speak, and let the others weigh what is said. (1 Cor 14:26–29)

Reading 1 Corinthians gives a strong impression of the perilous currents flowing in the turbulent waters in early Christianity. Trying to reconstruct the lost side of this correspondence forces anyone to move slowly. Surely what becomes most evident, however, are the problems in this early community. Enthusiasm always seems to propagate divisions and parties. The presence of gifts among these parties encourages Paul to seek some regulation. These chapters (12–14) give enough evidence that Paul did not think all was well in the Corinthian community. Supernatural gifts need to be regulated and their scope needs containment. The one Spirit is the basis of all (1 Cor 12:4–11), but a hierarchy should prevail in all these matters. First come apostles, then prophets, then teachers. The one body has additional functions to perform such as healing and speaking in tongues and performing works of mercy and even administration. Highest of all these gifts is charity.

For many Roman Catholics charity can mean the presence of sanctifying grace. For other Christians, charity might mean the acts of kindness to one another and to all. In fact the charity of which Paul speaks is the bond between Christians. Charity, both a theological and a moral virtue, should characterize Christianity. Enthusiasm, Paul knew, could create an atmosphere hostile to charity. Enthusiasm can often foster pride, jealousy, backbiting, and other forms of activity inimical to the unity that should prevail in Christianity.[4]

Such clouds of problems gathered on the horizon of early Christianity even among people who had experienced the earthly

---

ENTHUSIASM

I have called this section "Enthusiasm," not meaning thereby to name (for name it has none) the elusive thing that is its subject. I have used only a cant term, pejorative and commonly misapplied as a label for a tendency...

You have a clique, an elite, of Christian men and (more importantly) women, who are trying to live a less worldly life than their neighbors, to be more attentive to the guidance (directly felt, they will tell you) of the Holy Spirit.[5]

Jesus and the risen Lord, and who had heard the apostles preach. With such a beginning, why should anyone be surprised by the history of the Church? The same tendencies that appeared in Corinth reappeared again and again in the next two thousand years.[6] Frequently the ardent enthusiasts who favored the many gifts would forget the sober warnings of Paul to maintain charity above all. Less than a century after the death and resurrection of Jesus, the early Church faced the advent of heresies all based on enthusiasm. Enthusiasm was both blessing and curse.

■ Enthusiasm and Organized Ministry ■

The Acts of the Apostles in particular depicts the early Christian communities as a dialectic between enthusiasm and organized ministry. Pentecost surely manifests one experience of being *en theos*,[7] and Acts reports many little Pentecosts. The one most familiar was the experience of the apostles in Jerusalem (Acts 2:1–13), but then Luke also records the Samaritan's experience (Acts 8:4–25); Paul (Acts 9:1–19); Cornelius and his household (Acts 10:1–44) and many pagans (Acts 11:15–18, 19–26; etc.). The small Christian community lived fully charismatic lives filled with the gifts of the risen Lord and of the Spirit. The enthusiastic origin of Christianity created a community filled with collective inspiration rather than ministerial structure.

Eventually, with the delay of the parousia subsequent and the establishment of the Christian Church as an historical reality, the preaching of the Jesus tradition became better defined. Both Luke, in the Acts of the Apostles and the later writings of the New Testament progress from enthusiasm in the Spirit to the presentation of a structured Church.[8]

Many historical reasons exist for the change from a more charismatic community to one of a structured ministry. Often what begins in the Spirit ends in the earthly. Early Christianity arose from an enthusiastic movement, but even at the outset certain problems developed. For survival, Christianity needed to move to structure and organization. Luke depicts this movement very well in the Acts of the Apostles.[9] Since then, this same Church has regularly experienced similar enthusiastic movements in its history. However, there is no doubt that by the end of the first century Christianity had become sufficiently institutionalized. The heady wine of enthusiasm gives way to the water of sobriety. Such organization, however, does not mean that the Church is without spiritual initiative. The Church remains like the scribe in Matthew 13:52, able to bring the old and the new from the storehouse.

Enthusiasm lies at the foundation of Christianity, and enthusiasm causes problems. The institutional Church develops quickly as early Christianity moves from function to office. Disciples and apostles give way to Church leaders in deacons, presbyters, and bishops. Liturgy becomes organized and authority ensures a future. The presence of enthusiasm at the beginning, however, and its occurrence again and again show its need and function.

> Where wealth abounds, it is easy to mistake shadow for substance; the fires of spirituality may burn low, and we go on unconscious, dazzled by the glare of tinsel suns. How nearly we thought we could do without St. Francis, without St. Ignatius. Men will not live without vision; that moral we do well to carry away with us for contemplating, in so many strange forms, the record of the visionaries. If we are content with the humdrum, the second-best, the hand-over-hand, it will not be forgiven us.[10]

■ Groups in New Testament Ministry ■

The Church of Jesus Christ consists of believers who share a ministry. Each member of the community functions as a priest, according to the common priesthood of all believers, and as a servant. Each member continues the Old Testament tradition with its sense of election. Within this Church, however, certain ministries have been singled out historically as empowered through the Holy Spirit. In the New Testament some ministries are proper to all of the followers of the Lord and others are more limited to specific individuals or bodies of individuals. All can be called disciples of the Lord and can share in his ministry, but only some are called apostles and then, in an even more limited fashion, can one speak of the twelve.

Disciples:	followers of the Lord
The Twelve:	small group with specific tasks following Old Testament tradition
Apostles:	broader than the twelve, more limited than disciples

■ Disciples ■

Disciples *(Mathaetai)* is a generic term meaning "followers". The gospel of John prefers this term and uses it 61 times. Matthew uses it 36 times, Luke 12 times and Mark 9 times. The disciples are those who freely choose to follow the Lord, to be with him, and freely to accept a mission. This missionary aspect of discipleship becomes evident when Jesus sends out not just the apostles but also the seventy-two disciples (Lk 10:1–6). To follow the Lord implies a ministry of preaching the gospel as a missionary. Church ministry also involves leaders of the Church community. All have the generic mission of a disciple but some have a specific mission such as the apostles and the twelve, especially the ministry of Peter, Paul and the beloved disciple.

■ The Twelve ■

Mark states that Jesus chose twelve to be with him so that he might send them out to preach the gospel and give them authority to cast out demons (Mk 3:14).[11] Luke has a similar scene: "He called his disciples and he chose from them twelve whom he also called apostles"(Lk 6:13).[12] Matthew has no account of the choice of the twelve.[13] They simply appear as a distinct group in Matthew 10:1–2. The setting of the gospels suggests a new Israel fashioned by a new Moses. A great company comes from all Palestine (Mk 3:7); unclean spirits confess the sonship of Jesus; a high mountain forms the background, and Jesus chooses twelve to judge the twelve tribes of Israel (Mt 19:28; Lk 22:30).

No reason exists to doubt that Jesus historically chose twelve out of the group of disciples or that these individuals would function within the early Church.[14] In fact, certain passages in the New Testament, as mentioned, testify that Jesus gives to the twelve a solemn and continuing commission.

In the last supper discourse Luke combines the making of the new covenant with the institution of the eucharist and the commissioning of the apostles. In this account, Luke presents apostolic ministry in a liturgical setting.[15] The apostles will have royal authority or kingly rule (Lk 22:29). The authority within the community is expressed in the judging that will take place:

> As my Father has appointed a reign for me, so do I appoint for you that you may eat and drink at my table in

> my reign and sit on thrones judging the twelve tribes of
> Israel. (Lk 22:29–30)

Jesus gives pastoral oversight and authority to the apostles. Also in
this passage Peter will strengthen his brethren (Lk 22:32). The passage concludes with an implied sending out that is a stronger and
more strenuous campaign than in the earlier mission of the twelve.
This mission, according to Luke, is fulfilled in the activity of the
apostles at Pentecost. The apostles, the twelve, will teach the gospel
and bear witness to Jesus and will execute judgment as the overseers in the Church community, sharing in the authority of the Lord.

■ Matthew and the Commissioning ■

Matthew's gospel also has a solemn commissioning by Jesus to
the twelve as well as to Peter. In Mathew 18:18 the author uses the
term "disciple," but the context of this chapter limits its understanding to the leaders of the local church.[16] The gospel of Matthew
is often called the ecclesial gospel, since it so clearly manifests a catechetical, authoritarian and even hierarchical approach.[17] In chapter 18 the author will situate the leadership of the local church
within certain confines to make certain that these same leaders do
not exceed their appointed responsibility in the Church.[18] To them
Jesus will give a commission with the power of the keys (keys is
mentioned only with regard to Peter in Matthew 16:19, but the
same idea is present in the choice of words: binding and loosing).
The metaphor of keys that open and shut the gates of heaven is easily understood in a Jewish tradition. Those who interpreted the
Torah possessed the keys of the heavenly doors. Jesus is the new
key to the heavenly things, and to his leaders in the Church he gives
this power to bind and to loose.

Binding and loosing in rabbinic usage meant to prohibit or to
allow something, then to impose penalties; and finally to excommunicate or acquit.[19] In the Christian context, the meaning relates to
the forgiveness of sins. To enter the kingdom one must be forgiven
and must forgive. This understanding becomes evident in the words
in the fourth gospel:

> Whose sins you shall forgive they are forgiven, whose
> sins you shall retain they are retained. (Jn 20:23)

In the fourth gospel the power is given to the disciples in clear distinction from the apostles or the twelve.[20] The fourth gospel never

mentions apostles, and only rarely (four times, 6:67–71: 20:24) the twelve. But in the context of Matthew, it would appear that the evangelist would understand a specific order of ministry within the Church. Such an order would act representatively on behalf of the whole Church but would derive its authority and power from Jesus as the head of the Church. This is particularly clear in the conclusion of the gospel of Matthew:

> All authority in heaven and earth is given to me. Go therefore to make disciples of all nations, baptizing them in the name of the Father and of the Son and of the Holy Spirit, teaching them to observe all that I have commanded you, and behold I am with you always to the close of the age. (Mt 28:17–20)

Jesus chose the symbolic number of twelve apostles as the nucleus of his new people of God. He not only appointed them to assist him in his Galilean ministry of preaching and casting out demons, but he commissioned them to exercise his own ministry of ruling, feeding and serving the flock of God after his death and resurrection. The various accounts of this commissioning in the different books of the New Testament (Mt 28:17–20; Lk 24:48–49; Acts 2:1–4; Jn 20:19–23) do not record what historically happened but rather present the establishment of an apostolic ministry that has been stylized according to the theological understanding of the individual author. The twelve had a share in the authority of the Lord to bear witness to him as risen, to proclaim the gospel, to teach and to baptize knowing that he would continue to be with them in the exercise of this ordered ministry. Finally, they would execute judgment as the leaders of the new Israel (Mt 19:28; Lk 22:30).[21]

A reading of the New Testament gives ample proof that the twelve shared in the ministry of Jesus. The New Testament offers sufficient evidence that Jesus chose twelve. In the new Israel they would judge. They also had a missionary task. In fact, however, the New Testament offers very little about them individually. Only the first four mentioned, Peter and Andrew, James and John, play a significant role in the New Testament. The only one of the twelve depicted outside of Palestine is Peter, for he went to Antioch (Gal 2:11) and perhaps to Corinth (1 Cor 1:12; 9:5). Otherwise, the New Testament remains silent on the lives of the twelve. The image of them carrying on missionary preaching all over the world has no support in the New Testament nor in any other reliable historical sources. Archeological evidence points to Peter dying in Rome,[22] but the fate of the rest of the twelve lies hidden in the shadows of history, forever unknown.

Often in Christian history people have tried to tie individual disciples to specific places and proclaimed them as the earliest bishops. No evidence, however, exists that any of the twelve ever served as a head of a local church. Actually, only after several centuries are they described anachronistically as "bishops" of early Christian communities.[23]

■ The Apostles[24] ■

Usually "apostle" means the twelve, or the twelve and Paul. Such was the crystallized usage by the end of the New Testament period. But the word also has a wider sense in the New Testament. *Apostolos* in Greek means "a delegate" or "a messenger."[25] In the New Testament anyone given such a title receives a great honor, especially when a reader notes who is not given the title. Neither Apollos (1 Cor 3:5) nor Timothy nor Titus is an apostle. The latter causes great interest in 2 Corinthians 8:16–24 when Paul tries to commend Titus to the Corinthians in every way he can think of but is unable to call him an apostle. The *Didache* (11,3) indicates that at a later period itinerant evangelists were called apostles, but no such usage appears in the New Testament. "Apostle" was a more generic term than just "the twelve," but within the New Testament its use was limited.[26]

DIDACHE

In regard to apostles and prophets, act according to the doctrine of the gospel. Let every apostle who comes to you be received as the Lord. Do not, however, allow him to stay more than one day, or, if need be, two. If he remains for three days he is a false prophet. When an apostle goes forth, let him take only enough bread to last until he reach his night's lodging. If he asks for money, he is a false prophet (11, 3).

An apostle bore witness to the risen Lord (1 Cor 15:7) and had received a personal commission to proclaim the gospel. In Acts, Peter has a right to preach because he is an apostle (Acts 4:5–21; 5:27–42). Both Peter and John are apostles, sent out to baptize in the Spirit (Acts 8:14–16), and Barnabas is sent as an apostle to Antioch (Acts 11:22). Both Saul and Barnabas are apostles to the Gentiles (Acts

13:1–3). The term "apostle" was limited to a select few who had been commissioned to bear witness to the risen Lord, who could teach and baptize and, according to Acts 15, could also make decisions. As a ministry, apostleship is listed first in both 1 Corinthians 12:28 and Ephesians 4:11. The early Church valued such a ministry, for in fact the original ministry of the early Church was an apostolic ministry. When Matthias is chosen to replace Judas, Luke records that the apostles prayed that the Lord might make evident the one he would choose "for this ministry and apostleship" (Acts 1:25). "Apostleship" is used four times in the New Testament (Acts 1:25; Rom 1:5; 1 Cor 9:2; Gal 2:8), and taken collectively these references emphasize that apostleship rests upon a divine commissioning.

Apostles are commissioned by Christ and must be recognized by the Church or at least by other apostles (Gal 2:6–9). Their mission concerns stewardship and the preaching of the gospel with an ability to make decisions (Rom 1:1; 1 Cor 9:16ff; Gal 1:1, 11; 2:2). This type of apostolic ministry was not meant to continue throughout the history of the Church since these individuals were founding apostles.[27] No one would again take the place of the twelve or the founding apostles when they died. The apostolic ministry of the Church would continue through other ministries, but no longer would it be based upon a direct commissioning by the Lord.

Any attempt to understand New Testament apostleship will leave some unanswered questions. Since in classical Greek the word *apostolos* was associated with naval or overseas expeditions and was never used commonly for a messenger or commissioned agent, its use by the early community did not arise from common usage. A word had to be adapted to suit a new institution, but why this word was chosen remains unknown at this period of history. The Jews in the diaspora did not use the word, and when the new faith took roots in the west it was not translated into Latin but merely latinized.

Some suggest that New Testament apostolate represents a Christian development from the Jewish legal institution of the *shaliach*.[28] This word means an authorized delegate empowered to execute a legal or personal commission for the principals represented. If in fact this offers some roots for the New Testament understanding of apostle, then the apostles represent the Lord. The final commissioning by Jesus in Matthew's gospel makes clear that these close collaborators of the Lord will share in his authority and are empowered to act on his behalf, to bind and to loose. If Jesus had authority and power from his Father in his ministry, he shared this ministry with the apostles. [29]

■ Individuals and Their Ministry in the New Testament ■

Peter

Jesus also entrusted certain individual apostles to exercise specific ministries. The role of Peter in the New Testament has encouraged numerous studies.[30] No attempt to summarize these results of New Testament research is intended in this work. Rather, the focus will rest upon Peter as one who shared in the pastoral ministry of Jesus and how he exercised this ministry.

In the life and ministry of Jesus, Peter was clearly one of the earliest called to follow the Lord, but not the first. He was prominent among the twelve as evidenced in his name being placed first in the listing of the apostles (Mk 3:16; Mt 10:2; Lk 6:14). Simon Peter, however, did not function in solitary splendor. In the gospel stories he is frequently associated with other prominent disciples, e.g., James and John and sometimes Andrew in the Synoptic tradition and with the Beloved Disciple in the Johannine tradition.

PETER

Mark: first among the twelve; ambivalent confession of faith

Matthew: first among the twelve; clear profession of faith; rock on which the Church is built

Luke: first among the twelve; responsibility to strengthen his brethren

John: contrasted with the beloved disciple; given pastoral ministry in final chapter

---

Peter in Mark

Peter made a confession of faith in the Lord (Mk 8:29; Mt 16:16; Lk 9:20; Jn 6:69) during the ministry of Jesus. To evaluate this confession of faith causes hesitation since a critical analysis of Mark indicates that Jesus did not accept this confession by Peter. The presence of the confession ultimately accepted by the Church, however, attests to the actual profession in the ministry of Jesus. Mark offers a list of the apostles and places Peter in first place (Mk 3:14–19). Peter, however. does not figure as prominently in this gospel in comparison to the others. Mark, however, never seems to present the twelve in the best of lights. Mark does not exclude Peter from the lack of understanding of all of the twelve.[31]

Peter in Matthew

The longest version of this profession of faith is found in Matthew:

> Simon Peter replied: "You are the Christ, the Son of the living God." And Jesus answered him, "Blessed are you, Simon bar Jona, for flesh and blood did not reveal this to you but my Father who is in heaven. And I tell you that you are Peter, and upon this rock I will build my Church, and the powers of death will not prevail against it. I will give you the keys of the kingdom of heaven, and whatever you bind on earth shall be bound in heaven and whatever you loose on earth shall be loosed in heaven. (Mt 16:16–19)

Mark and Luke also have a profession of faith by Peter, but in these gospels the long section on Peter as head of the Church is missing. Certainly in Matthew, Peter shares in the ministry of Jesus with authority. Matthew, however, does not settle the exact nature of this authority. Although he singles Peter out for a special blessing from God that enables him to recognize Jesus as the Son of the living God, he does not distinguish his authority. In chapter 18, the other disciples also have the authority to bind and loose. Matthew also records Peter's weakness, for in this same chapter in verse 23 Jesus rebukes Peter and calls him a stumbling block. He who would be the rock upon which the Church would be built is also a stumbling block to the Lord. [32]

The authority and responsibility become clear in the choice of the words "keys." Whether this is qualitatively different from the authority given to the others remains moot. Also, some see this saying as belonging to a postresurrection appearance of Jesus that was projected back into the ministry of the Lord. The understanding of the authority given to Peter as understood by the Matthean church, however, holds more importance than the actual historical origins of this authority. Peter appears prominent in this gospel, and for this reason Matthew was used more frequently in a Roman Catholic tradition that stressed the apostolic continuity between Peter and the bishops of Rome.[33] But it should also be noted that the context in which Peter is given his authority is his recognition of Jesus as the Son of the living God. The authority of Peter relates to his faith in Jesus.[34]

Peter in Luke

Several passages in Luke's gospel are parallel to Mark and Matthew, but one passage during the last supper presents another image of Peter proper to Luke. Following the institution of the eucharist, he describes a dispute among the apostles (Lk 22:24) as to who will be the greatest. Jesus responds with a parabolic statement concerning the obligation of the leader to serve. Jesus then promises the apostles a place of honor because they have continued with him in his trials. Luke offers his prediction of the fall of Peter in a different context than Mark and Matthew, for here the apostles are faithful in the trials (Lk 22:28). Luke hints to their eventual falling away obliquely in verses 31–32, which form the context of the prediction of the denial of Peter (22:34) and his mission to strengthen his brothers:

> Simon, Simon, behold Satan demanded to sift you like wheat, but I have prayed for you that your faith may not fail. And when you have turned again, strengthen your brothers. (Lk 22:31–22)

The meaning of brothers here has a wider understanding than the apostles. The strengthening refers to his postresurrection role as described in the Acts, when Peter takes on his missionary role as the leading spokesman for the faith of the Jerusalem community.[35]

Peter will be the most active apostle in the Acts of the Apostles, and in that work he is given a role as a leader of the community. Again the role of Peter as strengthening his brothers is connected to faith. Jesus has prayed for Peter and thus Peter cannot lay personal claim to faith. As in Matthew, the faith of Peter is a gift from the Father in heaven. In Luke, Simon's role of strengthening involves a hortatory or missionary function, while the role that Matthew gives Peter as rock has the function of a foundation. The former implies a continual activity while the latter is a once-for-all function. The strengthening aspect of the role of Peter in Luke is parallel to the role given to Peter in the fourth gospel.

Peter in John

The fourth gospel contrasts Peter and the beloved disciple throughout. If the beloved disciple was not one of the twelve but still an eyewitness and disciple of the Lord, this can explain why he would not emphasize the role of the twelve.[36] If he also maintained an authority not based on the authority of the twelve, he would be contrasted with the leader of the twelve. In the epilogue of the gospel, however, the editor gives to Peter a share in the pastoral ministry of Jesus.

The threefold question: "Simon, son of John, do you love me?" (Jn 21:15–17) reflects Peter's threefold denial, and thus the scene is often referred to as the rehabilitation of Peter. The imagery is pastoral, implying an ecclesial role for Peter. The shepherd feeds his sheep, leads them to pasture, and protects them. Following the imagery in chapter 10 of this gospel, the shepherd enjoys an intimacy with the sheep: he knows them by name and they recognize his voice. Finally, following the same imagery as found in the good shepherd parable, the shepherd will lay down his life for his sheep.

The command to feed the sheep implies an authority over the sheep, but the context for this share in the ministry of Jesus stands out. Peter must love Jesus and be willing to die for the sheep. At this period of the early Church, certainly some individuals exercised authority over the members of the Church and no doubt some traced their authority to Peter.[37] By recalling the context of this authority, the author of the gospel of John specifies on what this ministry will depend: the love of the Lord and the willingness to die for the sheep.

Certainly the role of Peter takes on stronger tones in Matthew than in John, but in John it is stronger than Luke. The early Church also recognized some problems associated with the ongoing leadership. In 1 Peter 5:1-4, attributed to Peter, that author speaks to his fellow presbyters:

> Tend the flock of God that is in your charge, exercising oversight *(episkopein)* not by constraint but willingly... not as domineering over those in your charge but being examples to the flock. And when the chief shepherd is manifested, you will obtain the unfading crown of glory. (1 Peter 5:2–4)

The emphasis remains on leadership here as in the gospel of John, but the author also stresses the obligation toward the flock. Leaders such as Peter will have the example of the good shepherd as the model for their ministry.

■ Paul and His Ministry ■

Probably no other individual is more responsible for the actual authority and structure in the early Church than Paul.[38] The twelve fulfilled their ministry with their influence largely unknown. Careful analysis can distinguish at times the Petrine churches and can always recognize the Johannine community, but the Pauline churches predominate. Even the communities behind Luke/Acts and Matthew are closely related to the Pauline understanding of Church ministry. The study of the primitive structure of the Pauline churches shows more closely the development that began with Jesus as well as the development that has occurred from the time of Paul.

Paul saw himself as an apostle. His office was questioned at Corinth and he becomes defensive by proclaiming that he is a bringer of spiritual gifts (1 Cor 1:7), herald of the crucified (1 Cor 1:23; 2:2), the one who plants while another brings to maturity (1 Cor 3:6), God's fellow worker (1 Cor 3:9), a builder of the Church (1 Cor 3:10–11), servant of Christ and steward of the mysteries (1 Cor 4:1), father of the Church in Christ (1 Cor 4:15), and a genuine apostle who must suffer for the sake of the gospel (1 Cor 4:9–12; 2 Cor 11:23–28).

PAUL

Apostle to the Gentiles
Not an eyewitness
Not one of the twelve
Experienced the risen Lord
One who suffered for the gospel
Preacher
Letter writer
Church founder and governor
Jew and Roman

On the road to Damascus Paul experienced the risen Lord and because of this experience he claimed an authority equal to that of the twelve. Paul will also submit his gospel to those who were apostles before him (Gal 1:17). He will recognize their authority to judge his preaching (Gal 2:2), but he remains expressly independent and declares that he has received his gospel from a divine command through revelation, which no one, not even himself, can control (Gal 1:8, 12). His intention in dealing with the other apostles shows that he is not inferior to them and removes the question of the prestige of the other apostles from the relevant perspective of the whole mission of the Church. This perspective is the truth of the gospel. Whether unity with the Jerusalem apostles was a theological necessity or a pragmatic necessity for Paul remains unclear. But if he recognized the need to build churches, which of necessity would have specific structures and would have an identity apart from a Jewish-Christian church steeped in the Torah, he had to maintain a basic unity with those other apostles. They also were commissioned by the Lord. With them his apostolate was in truth in conformity to the gospel of Jesus. Otherwise he has "run in vain."

The Gentile mission of Antioch depended on the decision taken by the authorities in Jerusalem.[39] For Paul the essential criteria of apostleship are common to all the apostles. They are qualities that Paul shares in the same degree with any other apostle, even Peter himself. He went to Jerusalem seeking unity and presented himself as equal to the most important person in the whole Church, Cephas, and with him the pillars of the Church at Jerusalem. Once his personal authority as an apostle was established in conformity with the gospel, then he could continue his mission among the Gentiles and could in fact establish churches that would endure.[40]

Paul was conscious of his ministry and would not accept any subordinate role. He and his work, however, were still dependent upon the recognition of the Church, the source and center not only of the Palestinian Jewish-Christian church but of all churches. Paul does not wish his independent ministry to be misinterpreted, for he is neither willing nor able to deny the fact of dependence. He was conscious of his right to preach the gospel and declare the wonderful things God continued to do through Jesus. He worked to reconcile both Jew and Gentile, and finally he exercised such a force on the churches that he would be founder and governor.

■ Paul as Founder / Governor ■

As preacher and founder, Paul exercised a profound influence on particular groups of people. Spiritually he was the means by which the Spirit of God produced an effect on the deep layers of the personalities of his converts. Intellectually, his preaching caused a revolution in thinking, resulting in a modification of ethical conduct.

No longer would people live as individuals but they would form a corporate life assembled to worship, to pray, to read and expound the scriptures and to become part of the larger community. His ministry was based upon his experience of the risen Lord in consort with the Jerusalem church. Paul exercised his ministry by creating fundamental changes in the thought and behavior of his converts. He could describe himself as father (1 Cor 4:15; 1 Thes 2:11) or mother (Gal 4:19; 1 Thes 2:7b) who has brought them to life and let "Christ be formed in them" (Gal 4:19). Paul himself exercised careful ministry to all who would listen, especially the Gentiles.

Some may question the ability to understand the exercise of Paul's ministry since only his own letters remain. But precisely in these letters the reader can discover the kind of ministry he exercised when present himself and when acting through an emissary.[41] Personally, Paul exercised a power as a father and as a model. In some ways this way of acting is milder than a list of rights and obligations, but in other ways it demands more. How can one repay a debt of gratitude to the person who has given eternal life? Paul also exercised his ministry through his emissaries. They were to be accepted as having his authority (2 Cor 8:23-24). He expected obedience (1 Cor 4:17; 2 Cor 8: 23-24) and support (1 Cor 16:11). His emissaries shared in his ministry to teach, to instruct and to give leadership.

Paul also exercised his ministry through his letters. He admonishes, he orders, he commands; he reminds his readers that as an apostle he commands (1 Cor 7:12; Gal 5:2; Rom 12:3). As a charismatic leader Paul demonstrated by his actions that his authority rested upon that of Jesus himself, and although in consort with the other apostles, he preached the gospel independently. He would preach and reconcile Jew and Gentile. He seems to have liked the image of the one who nourishes, and he used every means at his disposal to minister effectively whether that involved emissaries or letters. He knew his right to govern, and he governed with a distinct quality based upon his own commitment to the gospel.

The Acts of the Apostles also offers witness that many early followers of Jesus, both men and women,[42] worked with Paul or even independently of him. Priscilla and Aquila provided a safe haven for Paul (Acts 18), and Lydia, the seller of purple (a sign of considerable wealth), seems to have headed a house church after having become a follower of Jesus through the preaching of Paul (Acts 16:14, 40). The long greeting at the end of Romans 16:1–16 mentions pairs of men and women. They were co-workers and helped form the earliest Church communities. Paul was an apostle who had experienced the risen Lord. He preached and founded churches, wrote letters, sent emissaries and built up the early communities. His influence on Christianity has remained.

■ The Beloved Disciple ■

The identity of the beloved disciple will forever remain in shadows.[43] As already mentioned, in all likelihood he was not one of the twelve. Probably he became a follower of Jesus in Jerusalem and was an eyewitness to the events surrounding the death and resurrection.[44] Unless he was an eyewitness his authority would be questionable, especially since his gospel takes an unusual approach to Christianity.

THE BELOVED DISCIPLE

Not one of the twelve
Disciple of Jesus
Eyewitness
Founder of the community
Inspiration for the gospel

The beloved disciple founded a community and was its primary authority figure. He taught his community the meaning of the Jesus tradition, emphasizing what he considered the essential characteristics of Christian faith: a personal commitment to the Lord and a profound love of the brethren.[45] His gospel manifests an approach to governance based upon this twofold approach to Jesus without the necessity of other teachers apart from the Spirit:

> The counselor, the Holy Spirit whom the Father will send
> in my name, he will teach you all things. (Jn 14:26)

> When the Spirit of Truth comes he will guide
> you into all the truth. (Jn 16:13)

Jesus alone in the first twenty chapters of this gospel has authority. The Spirit will share in the ministry and authority of Jesus over the flock[46] and thus the type of ministry manifested in this gospel could be called charismatic. The author, however, does not explain how anyone can know the presence of this Spirit. Surely the Spirit remained with the beloved disciple. Presumably the Spirit also remains present to those who have made their faith commitment to the Lord and demonstrate a love of the members of the community. They will even give up their lives for a single member of that community. The new commandment demands loving the way Jesus loved (Jn 13:34), which includes a willingness to die for the sheep just as the good shepherd laid down his life for his sheep (Jn 10:15).

The authority and ministry of the beloved disciple seems to have been questioned by the early Church, for the third letter of John reads:

> I have written something to the Church, but Diotrephes, who likes to put himself first, does not acknowledge my authority. So if I come I will bring up what he is doing, prating against me with evil words. And not content with that, he refuses himself to welcome the brethren, and also stops those who want to welcome them and puts them out of the Church. (3 Jn 9–10)

No doubt the beloved disciple claimed an authority equal to that of anyone else in the early Church. However, the mode in which he exercised this ministry in his own community seems to have been through a gentle approach to Christianity based on the essential elements. His gospel, unlike that of Matthew, does not end with a command to the twelve but with a testimony calling for faith (Jn 2:31).[47]

The final chapter of this gospel, added by an editor after the death of the beloved disciple, brings an understanding of pastoral ministry in the Johannine community to a conclusion. In this chapter, Peter shares in the ministry of Jesus by caring for the sheep. Three times Jesus asks Peter: "Do you love me?" (Jn 21:15-17). Three times Peter responds affirmatively, and three times Jesus commends his sheep to Peter's care. The context of this share in the ministry of Jesus, as already noted, establishes his ministry: a love of Jesus and a willingness to die for the sheep. For anyone to share in the pastoral ministry of Jesus, that person must be willing to follow the example of the good shepherd and die for the sheep (Jn 21:18-19). The final editor of this gospel would accept the authority of Peter and his successors but would remind those who shared in this authority of the conditions for its exercise: love of the Lord and a willingness to die for the sheep.[48]

The author depicts the beloved disciple as superior to Peter throughout this gospel: he reclines on the breast of the Lord at the last supper (Jn 13:23-26); he ran to the tomb first and believed (Jn 20:8) after he had stood faithfully at the foot of the cross (Jn 19:26–27); he

recognized Jesus on the shore (Jn 21:7); he never had to be rehabili-
tated, as did Peter, for he never denied the Lord, and was given a
promise that his testimony would remain (Jn 21:22–24). The ministry of the beloved disciple rests upon his testimony, which is the
gospel of John.

■   Offices and Ministries in the Early Church   ■

The study of the New Testament demonstrates that the early
community possessed distinct ministries and operations (1 Cor
12:6- 10), but unfortunately the New Testament presents only a
vague picture of these ministries.[49] Which were considered "orders"
or "offices" within the Church and which were functions remains
unclear. Not even the Acts of the Apostles give an accurate picture
of the ministry of the early Church.

Luke writes of overseers or bishops *(episkopoi),* presbyters
(presbuteroi), and deacons *(diakonoi).* Evidently the author pre-
sumed that the readers knew the meaning of the terms used. Now
readers can only attempt to formulate a more or less accurate guess
as to meaning.[50] The ecclesiastical polity can be understood only in
relationship to the historical development found in the writings of
the fathers of the Church, such as Clement of Rome and Ignatius of
Antioch.

In the development of the Church, the early local communities
came under the pastoral rule of *episkopoi* and *presbuteroi.* The
words seem to be used interchangeably.[51] Possibly the origin of
these offices can be traced to two different strains of Judaism influencing early Christianity. In Pharisaic Judaism, the *zeqenim*
(elders) set policy but were not responsible for the spiritual care of
the community. In sectarian Judaism, e.g., in Qumran, the
mebaqqer paqid (supervisor, or overseer) had a pastoral responsibility. Perhaps not all the presbyters assumed the role and title of
supervisor.[52]

The functions of these ministers also seems uncertain, but some
qualifications are found in 1 Timothy 3:8-11. They had responsibility
for common goods because they must rule their own houses first
(1 Tim 3:1–7); they taught (1 Tim 5:17), and they seem to have had a
pastoral role of shepherding (Acts 20:28; 1 Pet 5:2). Together with
presbuteroi and *episkopoi,* the early Church also functioned through
the ministry of *diakonoi* (servers) and *neoteroi* (younger ones). Again
both words were used interchangeably.[53] As an office this appears
only in Philippians 1:1 and in 1 Timothy 3:8, 12. They appear to have

been assistants to the overseers and were given authority to preach and baptize and are related to the seven in Acts 6–8.

---

episkopoi, presbuteroi: used interchangeably
    presbuteroi: elders
    episkopoi: overseers
diakonoi, neoteroi: used interchangeably
    diakonoi: servers for elders/bishops
    neoteroi: younger men, servers to elders/bishops

These principal ministers in the early Church continued the ministry of Jesus through appointment by the apostles. They taught, they baptized and they governed the communities. The New Testament offers little knowledge of their actual ministry, but some abuse can be detected in 1 Peter:

> So I exhort the elders among you, as a fellow elder, and a witness of the sufferings of Christ as well as a partaker in the glory that is to be revealed, tend the flock of God that is your charge, not by constraint but willingly as God would have you, not for shameful gain but eagerly, not as domineering over those in your charge but being examples to the flock. And when the chief shepherd is manifested you will obtain the unfading crown of glory. (1 Peter 5:1–4)

The early leaders were supposed to follow the example of the good shepherd in the exercise of their ministry. The early Church would not lose sight of the ideal of leadership as exercised by Jesus and would remind those who would eventually share in this ministry of the conditions upon which it rests. No doubt some had abused their authority in the exercise of their ministry. The author of 1 Peter called them to task to reexamine their ministry and how they served the community.

■ Variety of Ministries[54] ■

In three places in the New Testament a list of ministries appears: 1 Corinthians 12:4–7; Ephesians 4:11; Romans 12:6–8. Corinthians speaks of apostles, prophets, teachers, wonder-workers, healers, helpers, administrators and speakers in tongues. Ephesians lists apostles, prophets, teachers, shepherds and evangelists.

Romans speaks of three functions: prophesying, serving and teaching. Each minister contributes to the Church and each one builds up the community by his or her ministry. These three lists hardly give us a coherent picture of the ministry of the apostolic Church, but they were not intended to do so. Each was written in the course of a practical instruction on the duties of churchmanship as these tasks were to be performed by members of the community. The New Testament does not offer the precise nature of the ministry of these individuals but only that somehow all of these ministries had a share in the one ministry of Jesus and that all contributed to the community. In these ministries, the Lord gave a share in his ministry "for the perfecting of the saints, to the work of ministering, to the building up of the body of Christ" (Eph 4:11).

I Corinthians: 12:4–7
- wisdom in discourse
- power to express knowledge
- faith
- healing
- miraculous powers
- prophecy
- power to distinguish one spirit from another
- tongues
- interpreting tongues

Ephesians 4:11
- apostles
- prophets
- evangelists
- pastors
- teachers

Romans 12:6-8
- prophecy
- ministry
- teacher
- power of exhortation
- almsgiver
- ruler
- performer of works of mercy

■   **The Exercise of Ministry in the Early Church**   ■

The early community continued the ministry of Jesus in the role of the twelve, the apostles and other ministries. In every instance, however, the ministry was based on the paradigm created by Jesus. They preached and taught; they forgave sins; they healed and worked miracles; they baptized and gathered the community together; they ruled the Church after the example of the good shepherd.

The rapid expansion of Christianity demanded that these early leaders possess the charismatic authority made possible through the communication of the Spirit. The example of the good shepherd offered an example to follow. The presence of many individuals in the Church community with various contributions to make to the building up of the body of Christ also explained how the Church developed.

Paul had to react to the authority of Peter or to the leaders of the Jerusalem church, but his motivation cannot be forgotten: he needed the proper authority to build Gentile churches and would not create obstacles for the inclusion of Gentiles in the Christian community. He wanted one Church. Paul himself was charismatic, an enthusiast, but also when necessary he appealed to his commission as an independent apostle and established rules under which the nascent Church could flourish in Gentile communities. He proposed to be a gentle father or mother, but he also recognized the need for his followers to assume personal responsibility, and he allowed many of his followers to become his co-workers in the Lord.

Peter exercised an authority as the leader of the twelve but apparently in consort with them. Since 1 Peter is attributed to him, he followed the example of the good shepherd in how he exercised his ministry, and tradition says that in fact he gave his life for the sheep.

The beloved disciple was also a charismatic and enthusiastic figure who founded and guided the Johannine community. His power lay in his testimony of faith in the Lord and the love of the brethren. Like the good shepherd, he wanted to maintain the ministry of Jesus through faith and love.

The rest of those in leadership in the early Church were admonished to follow the example of Jesus. They would exercise a ministry by service, nourishing the community and recognizing the contribution that each member could make to the building up of the Church. The model of Jesus remained, always based upon the Lord who gave his life in service for all. Historically one group, however, seemed to have suffered most in a loss of role in ministry—women. After the first few generations, the Church became increasingly patriarchal. The contribution of women, so evident in the early Church, lessened in leadership roles, even if it continued by example. What will happen in the future remains to be seen.

Study Questions

1. The foundations of the Church as known today can be found in the New Testament. Is this sufficient to understand the relationship between Jesus and the contemporary Church?

2. Enthusiasm is a blessing and a curse. Yes or no?

3. "Disciples" is a broad term that includes everyone who follows Jesus. Why is this word so important for the New Testament and for today?

4. The twelve were significant in the early Church? Why? How is their role continued today?

5. "Apostles" are usually equated with "the twelve." Since this is not true, how does this affect your understanding of the meaning of "apostle"?

6. What do you like about Peter?

7. What do you like about Paul?

8. What do you like about the beloved disciple?

9. Does each of these individuals also have a dark side?

10. Office differs from ministry. How are they related and how do they differ?

11. How does the New Testament offer guidance to the Church today?

12. How might the role of women in the Church be rethought based on the understanding of ministry in the New Testament?

Notes

1. Cf. A. Denaux, "Did Jesus Found the Church?" *Louvain Studies*, Vol. 21(1996), 25–46. "Historically the roots of the Church reach back to the earthly life of Jesus. In his ministry numerous elements can be pointed at which show that Jesus wanted to

gather the entire people of God anew and prepare them in view of the coming Lordship of God." (p. 45).

2. Cf. C. H. Dodd, *The Apostolic Preaching and Its Development* (London: Hodder, 1936).

3. The original meaning of the word derives from the Greek *en theos,* which means to have God within. Then it may mean to be filled with God, or possessed by God, or full of the Spirit of God. The word has in its origin a religious meaning.

4. Cf. R. Knox, *Enthusiasm* (Westminster: Christian Classics, 1950), 9–23.

5. Ibid., 1.

6. Ibid.

7. The Acts of the Apostles shows the development from an enthusiastic community to what eventually becomes a hierarchical Church.

8. Cf. R. Michaels, "The Model of the Church in the First Christian Community of Jerusalem," *Louvain Studies,* Vol. 10 (1985), 303–323.

9. The pastoral epistles continue this development. Because of the similarity in development to a more organized Church, some scholars have proposed that Luke was also responsible for the pastorals. Although a minor opinion, it shows the efforts to document the development from an enthusiastic community to an organized and hierarchical Church.

10. Knox, 590–591.

11. Some manuscripts add after "He appointed twelve," the words "whom he also named apostles." This should not be accepted as authentic.

12. Cf. J. Fitzmyer, *The Gospel According to Luke* (New York: Doubleday, 1982, 1985).

13. Cf. D. Harrington, *The Gospel of Matthew* (Collegeville: Liturgical Press, 1991), 135–139.

14. Cf. Brown, *Priest...*, 47 ff.

15. Cf. S. Kealy, *The Gospel of Luke* (Denville: Dimension, 1979), 414–416. See also Brown's analysis of the place of the twelve in the Acts of the Apostles, *Priest...*, 56–59.

16. Cf. E. Schweizer, *The Good News According to Matthew* (Atlanta: John Knox, 1975), 371; R. Gundry, *Matthew* (Grand Rapids: Eerdmans, 1982), 368–369; Brown, *Antioch...*, 64–70.

17. Cf. J. F. O'Grady, *The Four Gospels...*,155–160.

18. Cf. Meier, 70.

19. Cf. L. Sabourin, "La Remission des peches: L'Ecriture

Saint et pratique ecclesiale," *Science et Esprit,* Vol. 32 (1980), 299. *Theology Digest,* Vol. 29 (1981); Richardson, *An Introduction to the Theology of the New Testament* (London: SCM Press, 1958), 317–319.

20. Cf.O'Grady, *The Four Gospels...,*90–91.

21. Cf. Brown, *"Episkope and Episkopos*: The New Testament Evidence," *Theological Studies*, Vol. 41 (1980).

22. Cf. O'Connor, *Peter...,*207. The belief that Peter served as the first bishop of Rome can be traced back no further than the third century. Evidence for a single bishop presiding in Rome as already noted cannot be found prior to the middle of the second century.

23. Cf. Brown, *Priest...*; *"Episkope...,"* 325.

24. Cf. K. Rengstorf, *"Apostolos," Theological Dictionary of the New Testament,* Vol. 1 (Grand Rapids:Eerdmans, 1964), 407–445.

25. Ibid., 398–445.

26. Cf. Brown, *"Episkope...,"* 328; Richardson, 319.

27. Cf. Brown, *Priest...*, 73–81.

28. Cf. Rengstorf; Richardson, 324.

29. Cf. Rengstorf and Gregory Dix, *The Apostolic Ministry* (London: 1946). Compare these ideas with Brown, *Priest....*

30. Cf. R. Brown, K. Donfried, and J. Reumann, *Peter in the New Testament* (New York: Paulist, 1973).

31. In the heart of the gospel of Mark, 8:22 to 10:52, the three predictions of the passion are followed by misunderstanding on the part of the apostles. Cf. O'Grady, *The Four Gospels...*, 33–40.

32. For an interesting explanation of the origin of this section of Matthew, see Augustine Stock, "Is Matthew's Presentation of Peter Ironic?" *Biblical Theology Bulletin*, Vol. 17 (1987), 64–69.

33. I believe that Matthew used Peter as an example of a centrist approach to Christianity. See O'Grady, *The Four Gospels...*, 155–156. Such an approach can always be helpful in finding ways to relate the bishop of Rome to the college of bishops.

34. Cf. Brown, *Peter in...*, 83–101.

35. Ibid., 199–125.

36. Cf. O'Grady, *The Four Gospels,* Chapter 6.

37. Ibid.

38. Cf. B. Holmberg, *Paul and Power* (Philadelphia: Fortress, 1978).

39. For an interesting insight into the situation in Jerusalem, see P. Achtemeier, *The Quest for Unity in the New Testament Church* (Philadelphia: Fortress, 1987).

40. Holmberg, 183.

41. Ibid., 80ff.

42. For a brief presentation of women in early ministry see Marie-Louise Gubler, "Living Diversity in the NT Church," *Theology Digest*, Vol. 37 (1990), 115–119.

43. Cf. Schnackenburg, *The Gospel According to St. John* (New York: Crossroad, 1982), 375–388; R. Brown, *The Community of the Beloved Disciple* (New York: Paulist, 1979).

44. Cf. O'Grady, *The Four Gospels*, Chapter 6.

45. Cf. J.F. O'Grady, "The Good Shepherd and the Vine and the Branches," *Biblical Theology Bulletin,* Vol. 8 (1978), 86–89.

46. The role of the Spirit in chapters 14 and 16 is particularly important. The Paraclete takes the place of Jesus and teaches all things (Jn 16:13).

47. Some manuscripts have an aorist tense; others have a present tense. The difference has caused some scholars to see the gospel as a missionary document: "in order that you may come to believe." The majority of exegetes hold that 20:31 is formulated for those who already believe.

48. Ibid., 341–374. Brown, *"Episkope*...337. S. Marrow, *John 21: An Essay in Johannine Ecclesiology* (Rome, 1968). Morrow offers the thesis that the final chapter was written with an ecclesial tone to make explicit the ecclesial thought implicit in the body of the gospel. This writer sees the final chapter as the result of the death of the beloved disciple and the need for the community to come to grips with other expressions of ministry in the early Church.

49. Cf. A. Richardson, *An Introduction...*, 312.

50. Cf. R. Brown, *Priest...*, also R. Brown, *"Episkope...,"*

51. Cf. Brown, *Priest...*, 34; Richardson, 325.

52. Brown, *"Episkope...,"* 333–334.

53. Ibid., 335–337.

54. Cf. M. Bourke, "Reflections on Church Order in the NT," *Catholic Biblical Quarterly*, Vol. 30 (1968), 493–511.

5.

Ministries and Offices: From Community to Church

*T*he ministry of preaching, healing, casting out demons, and forgiving sins continued through the efforts of those who believed in Jesus. They had experienced the risen Lord and became bold in their proclamation of Jesus as Lord and Christ (Acts 2:36). Like Jesus, these first missionaries led the life of traveling preachers waiting in expectation of the speedy return of Jesus in glory. Originally directed to Jews, these Christian preachers quickly extended their preaching of the gospel to Gentiles. With the passing of time as the teachings of Jesus spread, institutional forms and structures became tighter. What began as a gathering of enthusiastic Jews who believed in Jesus before the end of the first century became a Church heavily dominated by Gentiles.

In recent years many scholars have attempted to fill out this development.[1] Unfortunately they all face the lack of "hard facts." Only possible interpretations and hypotheses have resulted. One fact seems clear: the Church, as experienced now, developed slowly. Accepting this fact gives rise to a theory that seems to make the most sense at the present time.[2] Christianity arose as an enthusiastic movement that presupposes a fundamental solidarity and equality among believers without master-servant relationships. Such a theory need not exclude authority and leadership and the actual exercise of that authority, but the basis remains forever solid. The baptismal declaration of Paul: "There is neither Jew nor Greek, freeman or slave, for you are all one in Christ Jesus" (Gal 3:28) remains forever the foundation of the Christian community.

The actual development from the death and resurrection of Jesus to the organization of the Christian communities of Ignatius of Antioch and Clement of Rome lies forever in shadows. Complete

68

historical records do not exist, nor does a clear sociological analysis. Twentieth-century believers have only the writings of the New Testament and some knowledge of Greco-Roman organizations and Jewish institutions. The former offer some possible avenue of development. The latter enables a comparison of practices in the early Christian community with its social and cultural context.

■ Communities of Christian Believers ■

In the common Greek of this period, *ecclesia* (church) denoted the assembly of the free male citizens of a city.[3] In Hebrew the assembly of the Lord, as already noted, was called *kahal*. When the Old Testament was translated into Greek, *kahal* was sometimes translated as *ecclesia* and other times as *synagogos*. The Christians began to refer to themselves as *ecclesiae* of the Lord. The term had many uses. It meant the free association of Christians assembled at the house of someone, as well as the various house communities of a city (the church that is in Corinth), and could mean the Christian communities in several cities. Finally, the word could mean all Christians in the world.[4] *Ecclesia* can refer to the actually assembly of Christians, the Christian group itself, whether local or dispersed as many house communities all over the world. For Christians of the twentieth century, to use the word "Church" usually refers to a worldwide organization. Such a usage would be anachronistic when referring to the New Testament.

ECCLESIA

Ecclesia means first an assembly. The word was not used exclusively with regard to the Church until the distinction between Judaism and Christianity became acute. The English word "Church" comes into English through the German *Kirche* from the Greek *kyriakae*, meaning belonging to the Lord.

The early Christians made the *oikas* (house) the pastoral basis for the early enthusiastic Christian movement: the *ecclesia* of the house of Aquila and Priscilla (1 Cor 16:19); that of Prisca and Aquila in Rome (Rom 16:3); the house of Nympha (Col 4:15). The earliest structure in Christianity followed the general unit of civic life: the household. Such a household contained members of the family as well as servants and slaves. Early Christian groups built their proper structure on already existing relationships, both internally (members of the household) and externally (friends, acquaintances, etc.)[5] Different households existed within the city, which also gave rise to various approaches to the Jesus tradition.

■ House Churches ■

The house in these early Christian communities provided the forum for preaching and instruction; they gathered there and ate and drank and celebrated the eucharist (Acts 2:40–47). Sociologically, the heads of these households were wealthy citizens who placed their house at the disposal of the communities. The communities themselves, however, consisted of various levels of society. Such a structure continued down through the third century. In the early fourth century Christians could have separate church buildings, but until then the basic unit of society formed the structure into which the early Christian community fit.

In Roman and Hellenistic society the father of the house exercised the authority for all. The structure in ancient times was clearly hierarchical with a patriarchal order. Initially, the Christian community broke up this hierarchical and patriarchal structure since the community consisted of brothers and sisters, united in one faith, one Lord and one baptism. This would have made eminent sense in an enthusiastic movement. Eventually the hierarchical and patriarchal model predominated as the Church developed specific structures even as early as the end of the first century.

As with any society, eventually these house communities faced the question of structure, authority and the resolution of conflicts. Who is in charge? How are conflicts resolved? Who establishes relationships with other house churches? Who sets the rules and how must they be followed? If anyone thinks that the early Christian community existed without conflict, they have only to read carefully the Acts of the Apostles and the letters of Paul and finally the other writings of the New Testament. Conflict may not have predominated, but conflict flourished even among the leaders of the Christian community.

■ Early Conflicts: The Council of Jerusalem ■

The first fundamental conflict arose in Antioch at the beginning of the missionary work of Barnabas and Paul. Christianity struggled with early divisions. The split came between those who saw the teachings of Jesus as a system of doctrine and a code of ethics dependent upon Jewish law, and those who saw the teachings of Jesus as a proclamation of the redemptive act of God in Jesus by which God opened the way through faith to justification and reconciliation. The former position predominated in Jerusalem under the leadership of James. The latter position is Paul's. The earliest conflict involves Jewish-Christian relationships as well as Jewish-Christian and Gentile-Christian relationships. During the initial period of the Gentile mission, no effort was made to coordinate that mission with the type of Christianity associated with Jerusalem. The Jerusalem community saw the Jesus tradition as an outgrowth of Judaism with its observance of the law. Soon, however, the law-free gospel of Paul and the Gentile Church came into conflict with the legal framework of Jewish Christianity. The dispute came to a head at Antioch with the conflict portrayed in Galatians 2:11–13.

The council of Jerusalem convened and determined that Gentile Christians were free from circumcision but were obligated to observe those laws required by Leviticus of non-Hebrews living in the midst of Hebrews. Harmony was restored and Paul was free to continue his missionary activity in good conscience, free from any harassment by those who wanted all Christians to first become Jews. All of this is recorded in Acts 15:1–2. Paul then continued his successful activity as a missionary. But for his arrest in Jerusalem, he would have continued his preaching. Acts may have erred chronologically but has recorded the successful resolution of the conflict between Paul and the leaders of the Jerusalem Church.

THE APOSTOLIC DECREE

Abstain:
from anything sacrificed to idols
from illicit sexual union
from the meat of strangled animals
from eating blood

Acts 15:20

Avoid:
meat sacrificed to idols
blood
the flesh of strangled animals
illicit sexual unions

Acts 21:25

The resolution of this conflict shows the beginning of some established authority to resolve conflicts. Church leaders assembled together have some authority over households of Christians existing in different and distant cities. The Church at Jerusalem has authority since James, an apostle but not one of the twelve and the brother of the Lord, is accepted as continuing the accurate interpretation of the Jesus tradition.

■ The Council of Jerusalem Revisited ■

The explanation given in Acts has long been the traditional understanding of the resolution of this conflict. Recently, however, another interpretation has been discussed.[6] The apostolic decree of Acts 15 was not the resolution of the conflict in Antioch as recorded in Galatians 2:11–14 but the cause. Following the hint given in Luke that the dispute between Paul and Barnabas, which resulted in their separation (Acts 15:36–40), was subsequent to the Jerusalem conference, then possibly the dispute at Antioch was the result of this conference. Thus there is no future conference that restores the unity that was fractured in Antioch. The scenario might be the following:

1. Paul goes to Jerusalem to see James, Peter and John (Gal 2:1–10); the result is that Gentiles have freedom and Paul is reminded to remember the poor. No other obligations are involved.

2. The apostolic decree is formulated (Acts 15); Paul was not present.

3. Paul learns of the apostolic decree and confronts Peter, Barnabas and the men from James in Antioch.

4. Paul loses. Peter and Barnabas and others withdraw from table fellowship with those Christians who do not observe the Jewish law.

Up to this point, Paul felt secure he was preaching a gospel with the support of the Jerusalem Church and with the support of the Antioch community. After the dispute, Paul lost his power base in Antioch, and as Acts confirms, he had to travel farther west, hoping to find acceptance for his missionary preaching. He later wrote to the Romans, modifying his views from the writing of Galatians, but still maintaining his fundamental gospel of freedom. The tension between Jewish and Gentile Christianity, which had been present from the beginning of the Christian mission, as reported in Acts, was never resolved. Thus Paul never preached to the Gentiles without harassment from those who disputed his understanding of the Jesus tradition. He may have ended his career as an isolated figure whose theological insights and emphases were destined for decline in subsequent centuries.

PAUL AND JERUSALEM

Around 36 C.E:	Conversion
Around 39 C.E:	Paul goes to Jerusalem and meets with Peter and James.
Around 52 C.E	Thirteen years later Paul goes to Jerusalem to meet with James, Peter and John (Gal 2:6b–10); the result was the decision that Gentiles have freedom and Paul should remember the poor.
Around 53 C.E:	The apostolic decree is formulated (Acts 15). Paul was not present. Paul disputes with Peter, Barnabas and the men from James at Antioch when he hears of the new demands beyond his original agreement to remember the poor. Paul's position is not accepted, and Peter and Barnabas and others withdraw from table fellowship with those Christians who do not observe the Jewish law. Paul leaves Antioch and goes to Galatia.
Around 54 C.E:	Paul writes to the Galatians his strong letter defending his law-free gospel.
Around 57-58 C.E.	Paul writes to the Romans, modifying his position with regard to Jewish observance.

Obviously the defeat of Paul at Antioch did not mean that he was eliminated from the memory of the Church. Acts portrays him as a hero, and his letters have come down as a chief part of the New Testament. He was remembered as an apostle, a missionary and a martyr for the faith. But his martyrdom remains more common in the tradition than his teachings. The dispute at Antioch meant that the interpretation of the Jesus tradition other than that of Paul became normative for Christian ministry. Luke in particular portrays this in Acts.

■   The Church after Antioch and Jerusalem   ■

In the Acts of the Apostles, Luke replaces the Paul of Galatians, and, in a limited fashion, the Paul of Romans, with the Paul who will compromise his theology for the sake of the unity of the Church and the Church authorities. Luke presents Paul as the theologian who gives full support to the apostolic decree as well as the one who dutifully returned to Jerusalem to submit himself to Church authorities (Acts 21:18–26). This will fit in well with the images of the Church in the later pastoral epistles. Christianity was quickly becoming an organized Church with a system of doctrine and a code of ethics rather than an enthusiastic movement acknowledging God's redemptive acts in Jesus present in a gathering of disciples.

The recollection of this unresolved dispute did not disappear with the composition of the canonical New Testament. Marcion, for example, seems to have justified his preference for Paul rather than Peter by referring to Paul's condemnation of Peter. For Marcion, Paul rather then Peter exemplified the true Christianity. The Valentinians also shared this view, accepting Paul as the superior apostle. Ultimately those who favored Peter were thought to be those who were right,or "orthodox." Further evidence might be found in Matthew 16:17–18 wherein Peter is exalted as the "rock of the Church." Perhaps this combated the self-exaltation of Paul and his authority in Galatians 2:11–13. The apostolic decree, with its emphasis on doctrine and ethics, was followed long after salvation by grace through faith ceased to be regarded as the touchstone of the Christian faith.

Paul lost in his effort to influence completely the theological understanding of Christian ministry in the early Church. The community preserved his letters but often interpreted them in a way different from his intention. The later Church even added to his authority the pastoral epistles, which clearly differ from the teachings of the early Paul. Although he may have lost the battle, Paul's teachings in Galatians and Romans continue to challenge the Church to recall the fundamental aspect of the Jesus tradition, which emphasizes justification through faith alone.[7]

For the first thirty years after the death of Jesus, the early communities struggled with problems in ministry, and often sought a resolution through organization and structure. These early communities also faced the thorny question of the relationship to Judaism and found themselves embroiled in a future that seemed to imply a long delay of the parousia and the influx of Gentiles. In many ways these conflicts remain unresolved. Even the development of the "Church" in the final third of the first century and the first quarter of the second century could not answer all of these profound questions. Certain decisions were made that developed into the Christian Church as we now know and experience it.

A system of doctrine with orthodox teachers and the code of ethics with careful observation became the hallmarks of Christianity along with an authority structure to help resolve conflicts, both doctrinal and disciplinary.

■ The Church of Matthew ■

The gospel of Matthew alone among the gospels uses the word *ecclesia* (Church). Scholars often call it the ecclesial gospel, and through the centuries the Church has used this gospel for liturgical and catechetical purposes. The Roman Catholic Church in particular has favored this gospel. Not until the reforms of the liturgy of the Second Vatican Council have Roman Catholics listened to the other gospels in their liturgy on a regular basis. All Christians have heard of the sermon on the mount. Few realize that Luke has a similar sermon on the road to Jerusalem. Everyone knows that Christianity has eight beatitudes (Matthew); they fail to realize that Luke lists four. No doubt Matthew has influenced centuries of Christian history.

The community of Matthew probably flourished in the 70s in Antioch.[8] The community was a mixture of Jewish and Gentile Christians. The author, probably a scribe, probably saw himself in this passage: "every scribe who has become a disciple of the reign of God is like a householder who brings out of his storeroom what is new and what is old" (Mt 13:52). This follower of the Lord realized that the future of Christianity belonged to the Gentiles. He also accepted the delay of the second coming and prepared for future generations by offering guidelines for an established, organized, and even hierarchical Church.[9] Once Paul lost out in Antioch, he retreated to Asia Minor where he could preach his gospel more freely. The gospel of Matthew represents a compromise conciliating the more stringent position of James and the more liberating opinion of Paul.[10] The law continues to bind but must be radically interpreted by the Jesus tradition. This compromise by Matthew continues throughout the centuries, and the Church flourishes when the effort at compromise and conciliation permeates its structure.

Matthew expects Jewish and Gentile Christians to live in peace. He begins his gospel with magi coming from the east to worship the newborn king of the Jews (Mt 2:1-5). He ends his gospel with the command to make disciples of all nations (Mt 28:19).

Throughout the gospel the author makes reference to Jewish traditions while being open to Gentile development. This wise Jewish Christian seems to have seen both sides of an issue and patiently sought resolution by compromise and conciliation.

The ecclesial gospel also becomes the pastoral gospel.[11] Luke comes down hard on the rich. Such is not the style of Matthew. The rich may find it harder to enter the kingdom of God (Mt 19:23), but they can always be poor "in spirit" (Mt 5:3). If not physically hungry, they can hunger after justice (Mt 5:6). Even the weeds that grow in the Church should not be torn out but tolerated with patience and mercy (Mt 13:24–30). The story of the coin in the mouth of the fish (Mt 17:24–27) also exemplifies this tendency to compromise. Although the followers of Jesus are not obliged to pay such taxes, this exercise of Christian freedom should be avoided lest it cause offense. This also seems to have been the principle at issue in the dispute between Peter and Paul at Antioch. Paul proclaimed that Christians need not observe the dietary laws of the Jews. Peter evidently went along but backed away when this caused problems. Peter preferred to compromise rather than destroy unity. Even in Church authority, Matthew seeks a middle position. He recognized the need for authority and leadership but chose Peter as his model because he was acceptable to both Jewish and Gentile Christians. He confers upon Peter the power to bind and loose in chapter 16. In chapter 18, a chapter directed in particular to Church leaders, he also confers this power on the Church.

THE CHURCH OF MATTHEW

Authority and leadership
Hierarchy and structure
Clear teachings
Established liturgy
Procedures for resolving Church problems
Bringing out old and new
Criteria for judgment: those in need

The community of Matthew represents a community with great respect for law and for authority. He also seeks conciliation and compromise wherever possible. In the past, many readers of Matthew looked upon this gospel as rigid. If the emphasis remained only on law and authority, the gospel would be rigid. The presence of the conciliating spirit changes an authoritarian gospel to one that recognized the need for nuances and compromise. Failing to see this second aspect of the Matthean community brings the temptation to legalism, and authoritarianism abounds. Matthew allows no such conclusion. Perhaps this is no better manifested than in his ideas in chapter 18.

Many scholars, as noted, call this chapter the ecclesial chapter of Matthew.[12] It begins with the question of who is greatest in the reign of God or greatest in the Church. Jesus responds by offering the example of a child (Mt 18: 1–4). The one who is dependent upon God and on others is greatest. The Church leader, the Church member who recognizes the need for relying upon God and upon the members of the community, is the greatest in the Church.

The next section (Mt 18:5–9) deals with scandal in the Church. All, especially leaders, must take care not to harm those who are most vulnerable in the community. Scandals given by Church leaders can hurt the most. Sometimes those who are weakest can be hurt the most and be lost to the community forever.

The chapter continues with an injunction to seek out the lost sheep (Mt 18:10–14). Both Church leaders and members must always seek out the one who has strayed and welcome that person back. The Church that cares little for the one member who has wandered off no longer continues the tradition of Jesus.

In dealing with discipline in the Church, Matthew offers guidelines. When problems arise, go first to the party involved and seek reconciliation personally. Then call in a few others. Finally the Church will decide. If no resolution occurs, the person is to be treated "like a Gentile and tax collector" (Mt 18:17). Some have interpreted this as an expulsion with the shunning of the former Church member. Brown differs in his interpretation: "Is the officially repudiated Christian now to be shunned totally, or is he to be the subject of outreach and concern in imitation of Jesus who was so interested in searching out tax collectors that he was accused of being their friend?"[13]

The final section involves forgiveness (Mt 18:21–35). Christians, both leaders and members of the Church, forgive without limit. The power to forgive must characterize Christianity more than the power to excommunicate. People will not turn from Christianity if it is too forgiving. People have turned from Christianity in droves because they found it unforgiving. The unforgivable sin is to be unforgiving.

The Church of Matthew needed organization to survive in a sinful world. Someone had to be in charge. Rules had to be made and observed. Structures had to be established. The presence of all such elements in Christianity must never, however, take away from the call of Jesus to the lost with an infinite abundance of forgiveness. The Church of Matthew never settled for black or white. Gray often permeates in life, and when things go askew, Jesus offers the example of forgiveness seventy times seven.

Perhaps no section of this ecclesial gospel has more to say to individual beliefs than chapter 25. This gospel that championed the need for order and authority and structure offers one criteria in the final judgment: "As you did it to one of the least of my brethren you did it to me"(Mt 25:40). The community of Matthew recognized the need for Church structure for survival. This same author, alone among the evangelists, bases the final judgment on who feeds the hungry, gives drink to the thirsty, cares for those in any way in need. The Church of Matthew is the Church that cares for its members and for anyone else who needs care and comfort.

■   The Community of Luke   ■

Chronologically, the next Christian community exemplified in the New Testament gospels tradition is found in the gospel of Luke and the Acts of the Apostles. From the opening prologue, the author centers on continuity. The believing community in the 80s must feel comfortable that what it accepts as the meaning of the Jesus tradition can in fact be traced back through ministers of the word to eyewitnesses to Jesus (Lk 1:1–4). The same continuity persists in the development of Acts. The gospel ends in Jerusalem. Acts begins in Jerusalem and concludes when Paul preaches the gospel of Jesus in Rome, "openly and unhindered" (Acts 28:31).

The sense of tradition roots this continuity, but the Spirit makes it all possible. Throughout the gospel and the Acts, the Spirit figures prominently. The Gospel begins with the Spirit coming upon Mary (Lk 1:35). The same Spirit inaugurates the Church at Pentecost (Acts 2:1–5). Seventy times Luke used the word *pneuma* (Spirit) in Acts. Peter and Paul in Acts are remembered not primarily for their personal exploits but as vehicles of the Spirit. The disciples must not look longingly for Jesus in the heavens (Acts 1:11) but recognize the power of the Spirit on earth. This Spirit will accomplish the spread of the Jesus tradition to the center of the known world. With the experience of Pentecost, the apostles become bold in their proclamation. Subsequently, all those who will become followers of the Lord will be endowed with the Spirit from on high (Acts

2:38; 8:15–17, etc.). This same Spirit directed Peter to the house of Cornelius, gave the impetus for the missionary activity of Barnabas and Paul, and is proclaimed as the inspiration for the apostolic decree in Acts 15. Paul goes to Rome through the guidance of the Spirit (Acts 19:21), and when leaving Asia for Europe, the Spirit provides presbyters for the flock (Acts 20:28). Every step in the development of Christianity, from a small group in Israel to the worldwide Church, results from the activity of the Spirit.

THE COMMUNITY OF LUKE

Continuity
Historical roots
Power of the Spirit
Hierarchy and structure
From Jerusalem to Rome
Concern for the poor and outcasts

The community of Luke takes pride in its origin and its accomplishments. The community moves from triumph to triumph until the gospel reaches Rome. All is made possible through the power of the Spirit who continues to live in the Christian community. Christians may walk tall, secure in their foundations and confident in the future. Setbacks are temporary, for no one can thwart the positive and forward movement of the Spirit.

Such a viewpoint of the Christian Church, however, has its drawbacks and even lacks some historical perspective. Triumphalism and success recur frequently in the annals of the Church but cannot be verified throughout the early period. Also, such an attitude differs significantly from the power in weakness that lies at the root of the Jesus tradition. Christianity did not go from triumph to triumph in spite of all efforts to whitewash failures, even that of Luke. A community of the Spirit makes eminent sense provided that community does not lay claim to controlling the Spirit, or to limiting the Spirit. If only Church leaders have the Spirit, if only Church leaders can interpret the Spirit, then failures are inevitable. The Spirit surprises and even allows one generation of Christians to pay for the foolishness of an earlier generation. Paul knew this well even if Luke offers a different perspective.

A Church of the Spirit in which all have the Spirit also causes problems. If all share in the same Spirit, then the Church needs neither authority nor leadership. This approach to the Church has led to anarchy. Luke tried to counteract this by introducing the need for authority and structure.

Luke has his approach to the future Church. A sense of pride and accomplishment is good. An awareness of the powerful presence of the Spirit invigorates. One approach, however, does not suffice. The Jesus tradition shines more brilliantly than any one facet or gospel of writing can reflect. Luke makes his contribution to ecclesiology and allows others to make theirs.

■ The Community of John[14] ■

The beloved disciple and his community offer specific understandings for the Church as it continues the mission to remain faithful to Jesus and his tradition. The unique approach of this community to Church should remain, just as the testimony of the beloved disciple will remain (Jn 21:23). Historically the witness of the fourth gospel has frequently proven troublesome to the organized Church. For many decades this gospel was considered suspect. Eventually it became part of the canon as an authentic interpretation of the Jesus tradition.

The community of the beloved disciple emphasized the individual relationship to Jesus and the love of the brethren.[15] These two elements manifest the essentials of the Jesus tradition. With them all else is possible. Without them nothing is possible. The decision of the author to tell only two parables (the good shepherd in chapter 10 and the vine and the branches in chapter 15) emphasized the need for personal faith and the love of the brethren.

The gospel also deemphasized the ritual of baptism and the Eucharist in favor of the faith foundation for these sacraments. Baptism by water makes sense only if the individuals have been baptized

---

THE COMMUNITY OF THE BELOVED DISCIPLE

Based on commitment to Jesus and love of brethren
Spirit alone teaches
Sacraments only if based on previous faith
Emphasis on love of brethren, which presupposes love of God
Charismatic and free-floating
Peter given share in pastoral office in chapter 21 with conditions

in faith by the Spirit. The eucharist can be celebrated only if the community first believes in the Lord and has committed itself to Jesus.[16]

Authority exists primarily in the Spirit. In the epilogue (chapter 21) the community accepted the apostolic authority of Peter but on condition that he love Jesus and die for the sheep.[17]

The Church of the community of the beloved disciple emphasizes individual faith, the love of the brethren[18] and an egalitarian spirit with full reign given to freedom, spontaneity and creativity. The weakness of such an approach is evident. The community did not survive in a sinful world. Structure and organization protect but can also stifle. This community makes its contribution especially in the face of the organization of Matthew and the triumphalism of Luke.

■ Colossians and Ephesians[19] ■

Whether Paul actually wrote Colossians and Ephesians remains disputed. If Paul did not write Colossians, in all probability it may have been written within a decade after his death. The style may not be Pauline but the content is so similar that some hold that Paul actually provided the thought but that it was written by a secretary. Whether Paul wrote Ephesians is also disputed, but clearly, even if Paul is not the author, the author knew the other letters of Paul.

In both letters Paul gives authoritative guidance to the communities. An awareness of the enthusiastic aspect of early Christianity figures in Ephesians 4:11, and no emphasis on apostolic succession can be detected. Instead of relying on leaders to deal with problems, both epistles seem to present the Church as a growing entity, a spiritual presence that transcends. The Church functions best as a loving community, modeled on the love of Jesus for his followers and an awareness of holiness. This holiness of Christ lives in the Church, which is his body being built up in love (Eph 5:30–32).

The Church as the body of Christ allows for a fluidity and an acceptance of many charisms. This suits the earlier Paul in Corinthians. The Church becomes more personal than institutional. In it people can experience and manifest a love similar to that which Jesus offered in his ministry. The love of a spouse for the bride exemplifies the love that persists in the Christian community. Even pain and suffering fit in, for through them the individual fills up what is lacking for the body of Christ (Col 1:24). As Christ gave himself up for the Church so do Church members do likewise (Eph 5:25). The personalized Church encourages people to give of themselves. This offering can then pass from generation to generation.

The author of Ephesians knew the other letters of Paul and surely was aware of the sinfulness in the early Christian communities. Paul frequently dealt with the failures of believers. Yet this same author could see the Church as a spotless bride, holy and without blemish (Eph 5:27). The mystical Church as the body of Christ must be holy, for Jesus is holy.

THE COMMUNITY OF COLOSSIANS AND EPHESIANS

Love
Holiness
Enthusiasm

These characteristics of the Church communities portrayed in Ephesians and Colossians present a lofty ideal: love and holiness. The structure of the Church is not as important as the mystical identity with Jesus. Whether Paul wrote these epistles or not, the basic Pauline theology continues. A more enthusiastic and charismatic Church community belonged in early Christianity. This same tradition would perdure in later times.

But enthusiasm and mysticism bring their weaknesses as well as strengths. Survival in an often cruel and sinful world needs more than just enthusiasm. Surely the New Testament gives evidence for both the charismatic and enthusiastic communities as well as organized, structured communities. Eventually the latter become the norm without ever losing sight of the important witness of the former. The pastoral epistles not only follow the development of Luke/Acts and Matthew but further the movement toward organization and authority.

■ The Pastorals[20] ■

The Church of the 90's produced other approaches to the community that would continue the Jesus tradition. The Church has moved far from the primitive enthusiastic climate in Corinth. One word will characterize these letters more than any other: structure. The expectation of an imminent parousia has passed. Christianity may well have a long life to lead, and as a religious movement it needed to preserve its traditions and its teachings. Apostolic succession offers the means for such preservation. Christianity needed structure and the author of these epistles had a clear plan. Written with the mantle of the authority of Paul, these letters offer a remedy to avoid disintegration. Presbyter-bishops must be appointed in each town. These individuals will guard against false teachers (1 Tim 4:1–2; 2 Tim 3:6; 4:3; Tit 1:10). The meaning of these Church leaders and how they exercised their authority has already been studied. They provided stability, preserved the authentic teaching of Jesus, and ruled their communities with power. They taught sound doctrine (Tit 2:1) and maintained continuity (2 Tim 3:14). These epistles arose in a moment of crisis as Christianity dealt with encounters with the larger world and settled in for a long wait for the parousia. The call for control and structure became the norm for most Christian churches. The presbyter-bishops alone teach, alone carry on the tradition, alone provide the vision for the future.

THE CHURCH OF THE PASTORALS

Organization, hierarchy, control
Tradition preserved
Concern for authentic teaching
Charism becomes office
College of presbyters
Ritual for ordination and passing on of authority

The laying on of hands mediates the charism of presbyter-bishop. Such ritual has its roots in the Old Testament with the ordination of Joshua by Moses (Num 27:18,23; Dt 34:9).

> Do not neglect the charism which you have, which was given to you by prophetic utterance through the presbyteral laying on of hands. (1 Tim 4:14)

> I remind you to rekindle the charism that is within you through the laying on of my hands. (2 Tim 1:6)

Nothing in the pastorals focuses more clearly on the change from the authentic letters of Paul than the use of the word "charism." In Paul's lifetime the word meant the gift of the Spirit granted freely with diversity to all Christians. Now the word became united with a human ordination ritual, the laying on of hands. Charism has become an office, an official designation, an appointment authenticated by ritual.

The apostolic delegate preserves the deposit of faith, teaches and governs. The charisms mentioned in 1 Corinthians 12:28 and Romans 12:6–8 become the responsibilities of the apostolic delegate. Such a designation does not mean that only such delegates can teach, but because of apostolic succession the teaching and leadership roles in the Church enjoyed by the apostle are passed on to succeeding generations.

The pastorals also establish a college of presbyters (1 Tim 3:1–7; Tit 1:5) who become associated with him in his ministry. Later, in the letters of Ignatius of Antioch, the presbyters become subordinate to the bishops, a further stage of development. What had been charisms of the Spirit in 1 Corinthians have become part of the apostolic succession in the pastorals.

The tradition passed on by the apostle to his followers changes from a living *paradosis,* a process of adaptive, interpretative tradition in which the apostle functions as one link in a chain, to *parathaekae,* a precious object entrusted for safekeeping, unchanged. The delegate fulfills his function by handing on what he has received. He guards and renders faithfully the message coming from the apostle.

Strong leadership with a central control has worked well in the history of Christianity, especially in the Catholic tradition. This facet of the Jesus tradition has shone more brilliantly than others. To some extent, for some Christians this is the only facet of being Church. The Pastorals offer much that merits acceptance and adoption. They do not, however, offer everything.

Christianity began with a loosely united group of followers of Jesus and concluded with a well-organized hierarchical Church, all within a hundred years. Along the way the different approaches to the Jesus tradition and its continuity have offered guidance and direction. Each understanding of how the Christian Church may function had its merits. These qualities continue through the centuries. The New Testament offers the foundation for any understanding of what the Church of Jesus Christ may be, for it shows what the Church has been.

Study Questions

1. What does the word "Church" mean to you? Does the New Testament offer you any guidance in understanding the meaning of "Church"?

2. Why are structure and authority necessary in life and in the Church?

3. Did an ideal Church ever exist? Explain.

4. How would you evaluate the opinion given above on the relationship between Paul and the Jerusalem Church?

5. Explain the strong points in the community of Matthew. Are there any weaknesses?

6. Explain the strong points in the community of Luke. Are there any weaknesses?

7. What do you like or dislike about the community of the beloved disciple?

8. Are the epistles to the Colossians and Ephesians realistic with regard to the Church?

9. How do the pastorals continue the development of early Christianity, especially from Luke?

10. Diversity seems to have characterized early Christianity. What might this mean today?

Notes

1. Cf. W. Meeks, *The First Urban Christians* (New Haven: Yale University Press, 1983; E. Schillebeeckx, *The Church with a Human Face* (New York: Crossroad, 1987); R. Brown, *The Churches the Apostles Left Behind* (New York: Paulist, 1984).

2. Cf. Schillebeeckx, *The Church...*, 41.

3. Cf. Kittel, *Theological...*, Vol. III, 513.

4. Cf. ibid., 502–512.

5. Cf. Schillebeeckx, *The Church...*, 46.

6. Cf. P. Achtemeier, *The Quest for Unity in the New Testament* (Philadelphia: Fortress, 1987). See also John F. O'Grady, *Pillars of Paul's Gospel* (New York: Paulist, 1992), chapter 3.

7. Cf. O'Grady, *Pillars...*, chapter 4.

8. Cf. Brown, *Antioch...*

9. Cf. O'Grady, *The Four Gospels...*, 155 ff.

10. Cf. Brown, *Antioch...*, 39–44.

11. Cf. Brown, *The Churches...*, 132–134.

12. Ibid,. 139–145.

13. Ibid., 144.

14. For a fuller presentation of the Johannine community, see

R. Brown, *The Community of the Beloved Disciple* (New York: Paulist, 1979).

    15. Cf. O'Grady, "The Good Shepherd..."

    16. Cf. John F.O'Grady, "Johannine Ecclesiology," *Biblical Theology Bulletin,* Vol. 6 (1976).

    17. Cf. Marrow.

    18. Cf. O'Grady, "The Good Shepherd..."

    19. Cf. Brown, *The Churches...,* chapter 3.

    20. Cf. ibid., chapter 2.

■ PART III ■

The Four Marks
of the Church

Traditionally four marks or characteristics have been associated with the understanding of the Church. The Church is *one, holy, catholic* and *apostolic*. While each mark has its own insight into the meaning of the Church, the four marks are also interrelated.

The Church as *one* depends on an invitation to all to belong, saint and sinner. The *one* Church is the holy and sinful Church. This *one* Church also must rest upon the Church of the apostles and transcend all nations and cultures, making it the *one* true and Catholic Church.

The Church as *holy* presupposes the one Church coming from Jesus through the apostles. The Church rests on the holiness of Jesus calling all, both saint and sinner, to salvation. The *holy* Church extends itself to all peoples, inviting all to experience the saving presence of God.

The Church as *Catholic* acknowledges one true Church that offers salvation to all, sinner and saint. The *Catholic* Church professes the same faith of previous generations, from Jesus through the apostles to all peoples of all times and cultures.

The Church is *apostolic* because it is the one Church coming from the apostles. Throughout the centuries, the one Church has proclaimed the same message to all, sinner and saint, in all times and places.

Each mark relates to the other three and together they fill out what the Church means for all peoples. Any study of these marks individually presupposes the other three. Together they form a pattern that has helped to express how Jesus continues to offer salvation.

6.

The Church Is One

The study of early Christianity in the New Testament testified to a plurality of approaches to Jesus and a multiplicity of Church communities. Yet the first characteristic of this Christian community is unity. The theology of the Church professes that the Church is one.

The council of Constantinople[1] in 381 professed, following Nicea, that the Church is one, holy, catholic and apostolic. Each Sunday Roman Catholics and most other Christians proclaim this same belief. These four marks of the Church distinguish the Christian community, even if people do not always agree on their precise meaning. When the ancient Church fathers chose unity as the first characteristic of the Church, they certainly opened a Pandora's box. Even in earliest Christianity arguments were made to accept many churches. Over the centuries the actual presence of many Christian communities, each one claiming to be the "true" Church, argues against such a characteristic. Why would the early theologians and believers pay so much attention to the oneness of the Church, and what might it mean?

■ Unity and Multiplicity ■

Unity itself as a philosophical concept causes problems. Does unity ever exist apart from multiplicity and diversity? Do they mutually interact? Does one perfect the other? How can anyone even speak of the unity of the Christian God and profess belief in Father, Son and Spirit, clearly a multiplicity? If plurality and diversity explain something of the nature of God, why not just say that the Church is multiple and many?

Presently over three hundred communities belong to the World Council of Churches. This does not include the Roman

89

Catholic Church, some Protestant churches that do not wish to be part of any world council, and the thousands of storefront churches that not only are prevalent in the United States but are sprouting up all over the world. The World Council has done much for mutual understanding but has never claimed to be in itself a world church. Rather, it is a "fellowship of churches which confess our Lord Jesus Christ as God and savior."[2] Even the World Council manifests more diversity than unity.

How can the Christian church be one people of God, one body of Christ? When the diversity and sense of separation and even competition among Christian churches seems predominant, does it even help to speak of unity? Why not just go for diversity, with each Christian community good and valid and true in its own right and no one Christian church laying claim to more goodness or more validity or more truth or more unity? At least that would seem to be more honest. But if the early Church saw itself as one even in the midst of discord and disharmony, then somehow the meaning of unity maintains its place and value.

■ Unity in Multiplicity ■

The Evanston and the New Delhi declarations of the World Council of Churches give some clues for an approach. Whatever is done is done for the glory of God, who is Father, Son and Spirit, and the scriptures give witness to this profession of faith. The one Church mirrors God who is multiple in Christian tradition and yet still one.

NEW DELHI DECLARATION 1961

The World Council of Churches is a fellowship of Churches which confess the Lord Jesus as God and Savior according to the Scriptures, and therefore seek to fulfill together their common calling to the glory of the one God, Father, Son and Holy Spirit.

Like God, the unity becomes perfected in the multiplicity, and the multiplicity is the resolution of the unity.[3] To understand the unity of the Church presupposes not only the unity and multiplicity in God but also the eschatological destiny of the Church. The Church today depends on what the Church is yet to become when finally the Church reaches its own perfection.

> And I saw the holy city, the new Jerusalem, coming down
> out of heaven from God, prepared as a bride adorned for
> her husband; and I heard a great voice from the throne
> saying: "Behold the dwelling of God is with men. He will
> dwell with them and they shall be his people and God
> himself will be with them. (Rev 21:2–3)

Many of the images associated with the Church appear in this passage as the final destiny: a holy city, new Jerusalem, spouse, people
of God. The emphasis remains on God, both creator and Father. As
God is one, so is the Church one. While living in human history, the
Church may suffer from all of the limitations of being a human
institution and still have the qualities of a divine institution. When
God is all in all (1 Cor 15:28), then will the unity of the Church as
the work of God the creator and Father become evident.

■ Unity Destined by God the Father[4] ■

If God is one and unique, and if the Church expresses in a
human fashion the presence of God, then the Church must of necessity share in the same oneness. The creator of all has brought all
into existence through the power of the word, and the Church
expresses in history the presence of the Spirit of God. All things
must of necessity find ultimate meaning and origin in God the creator and Father. The multiplicity of the Godhead finds expression
in all of creation and in particular in the Church.

■ Unity Accomplished by Jesus, the Son and Word ■

Jesus as the word of God in flesh (Jn 1:14) and the means by
which all things have been created (Jn 1:3) expresses in his person
not only the second person of the Trinity but also the unity of God.
Jesus prays that the oneness he has with God his Father may be the
same for his followers:

> I do not pray for these only, but also for those who are to
> believe in me through their word, that they may all be
> one, even as you, Father, are in me and I in you, that they
> also may be in us, so that the world may believe that you
> have sent me. (Jn 17:20–21)

Belief in Jesus unites his followers. All those who come to believe in
Jesus throughout the centuries through the word of the preachers

are united not only with contemporary believers but with all who have proceeded in faith and all who are yet to believe. The teaching of Jesus makes it possible for all peoples of every time and culture and historical limitation to become one with each other and one with God through a common faith. Jesus makes all of this possible.

When Jesus invited his followers to offer the bread and wine in his memory, "Do this in remembrance of me" (Lk 22:19), he enabled his followers to have a sense of unity through a common meal. All differences experienced in life can be left at the door of the church or at the beginning of the eucharistic celebration. Rich, poor, old, young, educated and non-educated, the powerful and powerless, men and women and children—all that separates stands abandoned and alone, while only what unites finds entrance.

Baptism, the doorway to the eucharistic banquet, also unites followers of Jesus with each other, with the Lord, and with God the Father of Jesus. Once water has been poured over the head and the words spoken in the name of Father, Son and Holy Spirit, individuals become part of the community of believers. Their faith is expressed ritually. The same ritual that goes back to the earliest communities and will continue to the end of human history transcends time and space. The one Lord of all, the one faith of all, brings about one baptism for all (Eph 4:5).

> For as many of you as were baptized into Christ have put on Christ. There is neither Jew nor Greek, there is neither slave nor free, there is neither male nor female; for you are all one in Christ Jesus. (Gal 4:27–28)

The pastoral activity of the Church that continues the ministry of Jesus also expresses and accomplishes unity. Evil and sin separate people. Jesus forgave sins and cast our evil spirits. The holiness of Jesus and the wholeness offered by Jesus to all brings a sense of unity that can never be destroyed. The Church, continuing this ministry, can reach out to all peoples in all times and places, and not only can forgive the sins of all but can cast out the evil powers and forces that bind individuals and humanity. Pastoral ministry overcomes racism and sexism and extreme nationalism and ethnic superiority and political and social pretense and the exploitation of all. The Church, united in its pastoral ministry, gradually unites all peoples under the one God. Just as the ministry of Jesus could unite all, so can the ministry of the Church.

■ Unity in Multiplicity ■

Finally, the unity of the Church depends on the presence and power of the Holy Spirit. Pentecost reverses the tower of Babel. In Genesis, people are scattered and unable to communicate with each other. They had sinned and brought upon themselves the separation that still inflicts humankind.

So the Lord scattered them abroad from there over the face of all the earth and they left off building the city. Therefore its name was called Babel because there the Lord confused the language of all the earth and from there the Lord scattered them over the face of the earth. (Gen 11:8–9)

At Pentecost, peoples of many languages understand each other. "We hear them telling in our own tongues the mighty works of God" (Acts 2:11). Faith in the Lord Jesus made possible through the gift of the Spirit helps people to understand each other. Language and nationality and ethnic origin mean nothing. The Spirit of God easily transcends differences, making it possible for people to become ever more conscious of what they hold in common. The one fatherhood of God, the one brotherhood of Jesus and the one community of love in the Spirit make the Church one.

WHAT SEPARATES	WHAT UNITES
Nationality	One creator of all
Race	One redeemer of all
Origin	One Spirit for all
Age	One faith
Social standing	One baptism
Economic conditions	Belief in the eucharist

■ Unity in the Early Community ■

In the same Acts of the Apostles, the followers are of one heart and one soul. "Now the company of those who believed were of one heart and soul" (Acts 4:32). With such a foundation they could have one social life:

And all who believed were together and had all things in common; and they sold their possessions and goods and

> distributed them to all, as any had need. And day by day
> attending the temple together and breaking bread in
> their homes, they partook of food with glad and generous
> hearts, praising God and having favor with all the peo-
> ple. And the Lord added to their number day by day those
> who were being saved. (Acts 2:44–47)

They expressed the same unity in their prayers and the breaking of
the bread, all made possible through the Spirit who had been given
to them.

Often throughout the Acts of the Apostles, Luke makes references to the community being together. Certainly this same Church
had its problems of disunity, as seen by Ananias and Sapphira in
chapter 5, but the overarching gift of the Spirit brought a unity for
the community. They enjoyed each other's company, joined by a
common faith and love.

Father, Son and Holy Spirit maintain unity in diversity among
themselves. The Church, through the gift and presence of the Trinity, continues the same unity. God is not yet all in all. But even
daily the unity to come grows stronger in a world in dire need of
being united. The Church is one because God is one. The Church is
diverse because God is diverse. The one perfects the other.

■ The Theology of Unity ■

The classic definition of the Church, arising from the reformation and formulated by Robert Bellarmine, situates the meaning of
unity in a more juridical sense:

> A society of people on a pilgrimage on this earth, united by
> the profession of the same Christian faith, the participa-
> tion in the same sacraments under the government of
> legitimate pastors, the Roman Pontiff holding first place.[5]

In this definition Bellarmine offers the three elements of unity that
have become classic among the apologists from the seventeenth to
the twentieth centuries. Clearly these apologists and theologians
placed the emphasis on the external signs of unity rather than the
internal dimensions found in scripture. Usually the external is the
expression of the internal. Here it seems as if the external holds the
preeminent place.

The context explains this position. The controversies of the
reformation period resulted in defensive postures for the Roman

Church. The same defensiveness continued through the revolutions of the eighteenth century in politics and in education and research. The nineteenth century had its own mixture of revolt. Only in the twentieth century did the Roman Church begin to become completely separated from political regimes in Europe and in the western hemisphere and more open to the debates of science and knowledge. Such a change also brought about an adjustment in the understanding of the meaning of the one Church.

Even with the emphasis on the external and juridical, however, certain elements have remained in understanding the unity of the Church: unity involves one faith, participation in the sacramental system, especially baptism and the eucharist, and some unity in social life. From what has become evident from early Christianity, the Church requires some legitimate form of authority, better described as a unity in pastoral ministry. In the Roman Catholic tradition, this type of unity finds its full expression in the allegiance to the bishop of Rome.

■ Unity of Faith[6] ■

Throughout the gospels, individuals come to believe in Jesus and their lives become transformed. The fourth gospel in particular offers a number of individuals who in one way or another, to one degree or another, accept or reject Jesus.[7] The outstanding believers are the mother of Jesus and the beloved disciple. Throughout the gospel others appear with a similar commitment but not perfectly, e.g., Thomas. The Samaritan woman not only becomes a believer but an evangelist announcing Jesus to others (chapter 4). Nicodemus

---

INDIVIDUALS IN THE GOSPEL OF JOHN[8]

The mother of Jesus: ideal believer
The beloved disciple: ideal believer
Nathaniel: the true Israelite
Nicodemus: interested and curious observer
The Samaritan woman: bold believer who becomes evangelist
Philip: Greek disciple
Lazarus: the disciple who has died but who will be raised
Thomas: confused believer
Peter: repentant believer
Man born blind: open to belief, bold believer

appears an interested observer in chapter 3. Whether he ever became a follower remains unclear in spite of his return in chapters 7 and 19.

Chapter 10 of this gospel offers a fuller parable of personal commitment to Jesus. The good shepherd knows his sheep by name. They hear his voice and follow him. He offers security and nourishment. He never confuses them with anyone else. He gives his life for them. All they need do is hear his voice and follow.[9] Christianity rests upon a personal commitment to Jesus. Sometime in an individual's life, this commitment must express a firm conviction of adherence to Jesus personally. Just to grow up with Jesus never suffices. The unity of the Christian community presupposes this individual attachment to Jesus and then to all he did and taught. Such a faith commitment, however, does not mean that everyone must have the full faith as exemplified by the mother of Jesus and the beloved disciple in the gospel of John. The fourth gospel gives evidence of any number of believers who struggle. Peter is the prime example not only in this gospel but in all of the gospels. Faith becomes perfected only when an individual's life is over. In the meantime faith perdures as an ever-renewing commitment.

■ Paul the Believer ■

The New Testament contains many other examples of faith in Jesus. Paul has his religious experience on the road to Damascus and becomes not only a believer but an apostle.[10] Like many other before him and after him, Paul lived a life far from that of a perfect believer. No one could doubt his commitment to Jesus even if his presence in the early Church probably offered as much trouble as gain to the early community.

Paul, perhaps more than others, wanted to have a Church united with a common faith and common gospel. He knew differences had to be allowed for Gentiles but never entertained two churches, one for Jewish Christianity and one for Gentile Christianity. The one faith in Jesus demanded one Church for all. Even his change in mood and temperament from Galatians to Romans can be attributed to his desire to maintain the unity of the Church.[11]

Throughout the New Testament, individuals make their commitment to Jesus and the Church grows. A common bond of faith unites Christians in a community in which they care for each other. Before there can be a common social life or a common liturgical life, or even a common life of pastoral ministry including authority and organization and structure, first comes faith. The various questions posed in the first chapter do not flounder because of a common faith in Jesus. Every Christian has this. The unity of faith transcends all of the churches, the denominations—mainstream, evangelical, charismatic and the storefronts—that arose like so many flowers in a vibrant spring. All Christians share a unity of faith in the Lord Jesus.

■ Unity of Worship and Sacraments[12] ■

The two great Christian sacraments, baptism and the eucharist, usually define the liturgical life of all believers. Even within the Catholic and Orthodox Churches, which maintain other sacraments, no dispute exists concerning the centrality of baptism and the eucharist. These rituals define Christianity. These two sacraments, however, presuppose prayer.

■ Prayer ■

Prayer[13] these days seems to have fallen on bad times. Many people do not find it as easy to pray as in the past. Some have given up the practice since often it makes little sense in a scientific age. And prayers often seem to go unanswered. Why bother? Why should prayer form so central a place in Christianity? Why should prayer be the legacy of the one Church and why should prayer contribute to the unity of the Church?

Traditionally prayer meant the lifting of the mind and heart to God, or, more simply, speaking with God. Prayer involves a communication and sharing with and listening to God. The Bible asserts that all prayer rests on the belief that God is near and interested in every aspect of human life.

■ Prayer and the Old Testament ■

In the ancient past, some peoples viewed prayer as magic: they could control God by performing certain rituals, repeating some incantations. The Bible opposes all magic in prayer. Israel founded its prayer on the experience of the presence of God as powerful and gracious and who had promised to bless the people (Gen 26:3). This gracious God looked into the hearts of people seeking "a contrite and humble heart" (Ps 51:19).

Prayer in the Old Testament has three aspects: the memory of the past when God had been good to the people of Israel—God delivered them from bondage (Ex 12:37ff); the present—"He will not forget his covenant" (Deut 4:31); the future coming of God (Ez 20:39–44).

I will give you a new heart and place a new spirit within
you, taking from your bodies your stony hearts and giving you natural hearts. (Ez 36:26)

God was faithful in the past. This encourages prayer in the present
as people await a final and complete presence of God in their lives in
the future. God pulsates in every aspect of human life. Faithful
believers could turn to their God for assistance, for they knew God
had blessed them in the past and would be with them forever.

■ Prayer and the New Testament ■

The New Testament continues these same traditions of
prayer. Jesus taught his disciples to pray. Frequently they would
withdraw together to pray to God. Jesus, however, seems to have
done this more frequently than anyone else. He prayed before the
principal events in his ministry: in his baptism, before he chose the
twelve apostles, after he had ministered to people through his healing, at the last supper, in the garden, and on the cross. Jesus felt the
need to lift his mind and heart to God, to speak to the God whom he
also called "Abba," "Father."

The gospel writers all portray an intimate relationship between
Jesus and God. He felt at ease when he prayed and evidently could
feel free to pray for anything, even for deliverance from a painful
death. He prayed most often for others, a lesson for his followers.

As a Jew, Jesus knew that his God had been faithful in the
past and would continue to be faithful in the present and in the
future. God had blessed him and so Jesus could die with confidence,
for he could entrust himself into the hand of a loving God: "Father,
into your hands I commend my spirit" (Lk 23:46).

When he taught his disciples to pray, he told them to call God
"Abba," "Father." In the Lord's prayer he instructed them to begin by
praising God for his goodness with a hope for the recognition of the
presence of God by all people. This prayer, the model of all prayer,
continues with praying for all daily needs, asking for forgiveness and
promising to offer forgiveness to others, and, finally, begging God to
preserve all from the power of evil.[14] Prayer unites all Christians.

■ Baptism[15] ■

Christians usually view baptism as a once-for-all ceremony.
Parents take a newborn to church, the Church community welcomes the child, the priest pours water over the infant's head and

the baby is now baptized. But baptism is more than just a ceremony from the past. Baptism marks the start of the Christian life, the journey of each day trying to live a life fashioned on the example of Jesus until human life is over.

The gospels of Matthew, Mark and Luke record the baptism of Jesus. The gospel of John does not actually mention the event but seems to imply it. Jesus accepted a pouring of water for repentance at the hands of John the Baptist, and then, filled with the Spirit, he began his ministry.

THE BAPTISM OF JESUS

Jesus came from Nazareth in Galilee and was baptized in the Jordan by John. Immediately on coming up out of the water he saw the sky rent in two and the Spirit descending on him like a dove. Then a voice came from the heavens: "You are my beloved Son. On you my favor rests." (Mk 1:9–11)

Later Jesus coming from Galilee appeared before John at the Jordan to be baptized by him. John tried to refuse him by the protest, "I should be baptized by you, yet you come to me!" Jesus answered, "Give in for now. We must do this if we would fulfill all of God's demands." So John gave in. After Jesus was baptized he came directly out of the water. Suddenly the sky opened and he saw the Spirit of God descend like a dove and hover over him. With that a voice from the heavens said, "This is my beloved Son. My favor rest on him." (Mt 3:13–17)

When all the people were baptized, and Jesus was at prayer after likewise being baptized, the sky opened and the Holy Spirit descended on him in visible form like a dove. A voice from heaven was heard to say:" You are my beloved Son. On you my favor rests." (Lk 3:21–22)

Christians do not presume that Jesus ever needed a baptism for the remission of sins. But such a belief should not downplay the importance of baptism in the life of Jesus. The baptism inaugurated his ministry, and that surely had great significance for both Jesus and his followers. The coming of the Spirit upon Jesus and the resting upon him shows the extraordinary person involved and helps us to understand the meaning of baptism.

Jesus came out of the water and began to preach the reign of God. God was present in human life and loved all people. When he began his ministry, Jesus started a journey that would lead to the cross and the outpouring of the Spirit on humanity. On Pentecost when Peter preached, those who listened also received the Spirit. John prophesied that another would come after him who would baptize with the Spirit. The crucified and risen Lord poured out the Spirit on the disciples at Pentecost, and they in turn preached and the Spirit was given. Baptism means being blessed and filled with the Holy Spirit.

The early Christians also knew that allowing the Spirit of God to influence them was a lifelong event. Overcoming evil and the conquest of sin involved a daily struggle. Being filled with the Spirit meant allowing the presence of God to fill up all the facets of the human personality, not picking and choosing but being open to all God desires. Spirit-filled people give of themselves to God and to others. They are holy, for God is with them and in them. Paul could remark: "It is no longer I that live, but Christ who lives in me" (Gal 2:20).

The one baptism of Christianity begins a process for all Christians. People are born into a world, move through life, and then die. Birth is a beginning of dying. With baptism, Christians enter into the life of faith. They move through life filled with the Holy Spirit. Gradually believers respond to the presence of God to overcome the evil and sin in every human life. The process takes a lifetime and finds completion when the individuals give of themselves in death into the hands of a loving God.

Baptism also begins the life of the believer as a member of the Church, where individuals collectively help each other to overcome evil and sin. Guided by the Word of God and with the assistance of the sacrament's and prayer, people become part of the community of faith. The Christian life contains its share of struggle, but united with others, believers experience the joy of the Spirit of God that builds up the Church, making it a tangible sign of the presence of God in the world today.

Baptism may be related to sin, not only in the sense of original sin but rather being filled with the love of God that destroys all sin. The effects of baptism not only concern original sin but help in the struggle against all evil and sin. People are born into a sinful environment, contribute to this evil environment by personal sin and lack the fullness of God's presence. Baptism begins the process that will overcome this human legacy.

The unity of one baptism helps individual Christians to recognize their common call to holiness. People are often afraid to open themselves to God and to others for fear of losing what one already has. Christians take a chance to trust God to heal the bitterness and the hurt of unhappy memories that form part of everyone's past. The result amazes, for instead of losing, people gain what they had rarely ever hoped to gain.

Baptism begins the process of faith, the start of living in faith that finds its completion only in death. All are destined to live and all are destined to die. baptism initiates the life of faith that persists through human life and finds completion in death. Baptism unites all Christians.

■ The Eucharist[16] ■

The Passover made the ancient Jews a people, united with a common faith, under the protection of one God. Of the many meanings and symbolism associated with the eucharist, the eucharist as Christian Passover stands out as primary. All of the sources affirm that the last supper was—at least was like—a Passover dinner for Jesus and his disciples, even if John places it on the evening before Passover. The Passover commemorated the powerful saving event of the Old Testament, the exodus, in ritual. The eucharist commemorates the great saving event of Jesus, his death and resurrection, in the New Testament.

The ancient priestly source of the Pentateuch places the first Passover in Egypt with a supper anticipating the event which will follow. The new Christian Passover, the death and resurrection of Jesus, is also anticipated by an evening supper. The passover from Egypt to the desert and to the promised land, with salvation and freedom and the origin of a people, has its counterpart as Jesus moves from life to death to resurrected life offering salvation and freedom and making a new people.

■ The New Passover ■

Jesus sacrifices himself for the sake of his disciples, thus making it possible for them to live not only reconciled with God, but at peace with themselves and with all others. The paschal lamb never had a sacrificial tone in the Old Testament, and even in the formulation of the institution of the eucharist the sacrificial tone appears only implicit, but atonement is present. The body and blood are "for many," "for you." The eucharist is the memorial (Lk 22:19; 1 Cor 11:24), proclaiming the atoning death (1 Cor 11:26). The cultic and ritual enactment of the death of Jesus makes it possible for all participants to experience the event. The individual becomes integrated into the death and resurrection of Jesus. The sacrificial element is also found in 1 Corinthians 10:14–22. Through the ritual meal people become united to the divine. The sacramental presence of Jesus makes this possible. If people are to be united to God and if people have material as well as spiritual dimensions, then the material, the physical, must be the means by which the union is accomplished.

Just how the bread and wine become the body and blood of Jesus remains a mystery. Centuries of theological speculation have offered many theories to protect against misunderstanding. Whatever the explanation, the belief in the real presence of Jesus in this ritual meal has characterized Christianity from its origins.

The word "eucharist," from the Greek word meaning "thanksgiving," designates the ritual of a sacred meal commemorating the death and resurrection of Jesus. The word does not appear in the New Testament. The first time the word appears in ancient Christian tradition is in the late first-century or early second-century document, the *Didache*. In this same time period, the word also appears in Ignatius of Antioch and Justin Martyr. The New Testament prefers "the Lord's Supper" or the "breaking of the bread."[17] The rite, however, surely existed in the beginning of the Christian community. Also, no doubt exists with regard to the centrality of this cult in primitive Christianity. Every religion needs its rituals, and the eucharist fulfilled this need for the earliest communities as it does today.

In regard to the Eucharist, you shall give thanks thus: First in regard to the cup: We give you thanks, our Father, for the holy vine of David your son, which you have made known to us through Jesus your Son. Glory be to you forever. In regard to the broken bread: We give you thanks, our Father, for the life and knowledge which you have made known to us through Jesus your Son. Glory be to you forever. As this broken bread was scattered on the mountains, but brought together was made one, so gather your Church from the ends of the earth into your kingdom.

Didache 9,1

■ The Eucharist and Unity ■

Paul speaks of the Church as the body of Christ. If the eucharist makes it possible for believers to experience in a personal and communal way the body of Christ in sacramental form, then the eucharist creates an effective sign of Christian unity. Originally it seems that the eucharist was united with a communal meal (1 Cor 11:17–33). The same is implied in Acts 2:46. The eucharist is a participation in the body of Christ in which Christians are all one. The many are one body, for they partake of the one bread (1 Cor 10:17). Quickly the ritual meal became separated from a common meal. This would emphasize its distinctive and sacred character, a meal that makes the Lord present and unites all.

Prayer, baptism and the celebration of the eucharist not only express the unity of the Church but actually effect this unity. Sacraments express a reality already present. The Church is one through the gift of God, creator, Father, Son and Holy Spirit. The unity already existing finds expression in both worship and ritual. The result of this repeated behavior adds to and enhances the unity. Where people gather together in the name of Jesus, there is Jesus (Mt 18:20). One Lord, one faith, one baptism (Eph 4:5) and one sacred meal offered for all make the Christian Church ever more united.

■ Unity of Social Life[18] ■

The end, the purpose, the rule of the Christian community remains charity, the love of the brethren fashioned after the example of Jesus who gave his life for the sheep (Jn 10:11). Charity, love, pulsates through the Christian community as a force that gathers the multiplicity of individuals, of human endeavors, of hopes and accomplishments into unity. The differences remain. Charity not only allows for differences but celebrates them. Under the umbrella of love, individuals maintain their individuality with personal hopes and expectations but still unite with others similarly disposed.

The charity of service functions as the foundation. Jesus came not to be served but to serve (Mk 10:45). As Jesus gave his life for others, so the love within the community encourages people to give of themselves to each other. No greater love does one have than to give one's life for a friend (Jn 15:13). The one who loses his life for others finds that life (Mk 8:35). People never lose when they give of themselves. The love given returns tenfold. The many gifts within the community serve each other (1 Cor 12:4–5; Eph 4:12). People in the Church cooperate; they work together for the good of each other.

Individuals can count on those who share a common faith. The charity of service makes the Church alive.

In Christian tradition, those who believe in Jesus act for one another. The communion of saints not only makes communication possible but also bestows the ability to act in favor of the other. When people do not communicate honestly, troubles brew; communication breaks down. But if charity persists among people, then this common bond makes communication possible and successful. The Holy Spirit vivifies the community with powerful love. With this basis, people can function for each other without being self-serving.

The charity of a shared life also exalts the unity of the Church. Different members do different things. Preaching presupposes preachers. Baptism needs catechesis, as does the eucharist. A shared life with each person giving and receiving based on a mutual love exhilarates the Church community. The unity depends on the differences serving the one community of faith.

■ Unity of Pastoral Ministry[19] ■

Any community needs leadership. The survival of the Christian Church depended on effective leaders who were first disciples. The New Testament, as already seen, contains numerous examples of the authority structure in the early Church. From Matthew to Luke/Acts to the pastorals, early Christianity developed its own system of governance.

The example remains the good shepherd, who not only guides but nourishes and willingly dies for the sheep. The love of Jesus sustains any Christian pastoral minister. Presbyters and overseers and deacons of old have given way to deacons, priests, bishops and pope today. They continue to teach and preach, to manage the household of the saints, to correct and admonish, and always in love.

Leadership in the Christian Church contributes to unity by holding the disparate elements together. Each is both sign and cause of unity. The unity already exists through God's gift, through prayer and worship and ritual and through a shared life of charity. All of these are supported by directions, guidelines, rules, commandments, regular meetings and someone in charge. The unity of pastoral service can only enhance the presence of charity, provided it always follows the example of the good shepherd.

■ The Church as One and Multiple[20] ■

The Christian Church flourishes as a communion. The unity
does not imply uniformity. God gives as God wills, and the multiplicity and community in God will be reflected in the multiplicity
and differences in the Church. The universal Church is the spouse
(Eph 5:23); the local church is the spouse (2 Cor 11:2–3); the individual is the spouse (1 Cor 6:15–17). The multiplicity with all of the differences does not maim the unity. The individual, the local
community, and the universal Church are all united as the spouse
of the Lord.

The individual and local church and the universal Church
share a common task, a responsibility, a common defense and a
common mission. They live in community (1 Cor 10:16; 2 Cor
13:11–14). The concord and harmony create a spiritual and moral
union to achieve a fellowship with all. The many different elements
in the history of the Church, whether they be councils, encyclicals,
creeds, feasts or blessings, all contribute to the unity of hearts. The
unity remains always to be accomplished, since ultimately it looks
to the day when God will be all in all (1 Cor 15:28).

In spite of the many churches, the divisions, the differences,
even the seeming contradictions, the Church remains one. The one
God has created the Church through the activity of Father, Son and
Spirit. The individual believers share a common faith, common ritual and a common Christian life. With these foundations all the differences can find resolution. In an age when ecumenism seems on
the wane, the reassertion of what unites can only help. The Church
remains one.

■ Breaking of Unity[21] ■

Only someone who suffers from a lack of all historical awareness and lives in a fantasy world could ever maintain that the
Christian church has always existed as one. From the very outset,
the scriptural and theological meaning of unity lies shattered not
only in the pages of history but before every doorway to every Christian church. The Christian church is not one. Broken pieces characterize its history more so than an institution of love and faith.

Some might live under the illusion that all was in perfect order
in the earliest of Christian communities. The Acts of the Apostles,
and the letters of Paul, especially Galatians and 1 and 2 Corinthians, destroys that illusion. Even the later writings of the New Testament, the pastorals, the letter of James, all point to dissensions,

quarrels, separations, jealousies, rivalries, accusations and every manner of sin that would almost destroy any hope of unity.

The differences so nicely discussed in both scripture and theology, the various ministries, with each person making a contribution to build up the whole, are rather disruptive divisions.The differences often do not build up the unity but further splinter and divide. All the beautiful theology of unity falls apart in the present reality of the Christian Church.

If faith and love, personal commitment to Jesus and love of the brethren are the hallmarks of the community that built up unity, the lack of these tear down the Church and its hoped-for unity. Schism destroys the love that should bind Christians together and heresy destroys the understanding of faith.

■ Schism ■

Schism ruptures love, especially the communion with a common eucharist. East and west have broken communion. On June 29, 1995, the patriarch of Constantinople, Bartholomew, and the patriarch of the west, Pope John Paul II, joined together to celebrate the feast of Saints Peter and Paul. Each offered thoughts and prayers in their respective homilies. At the end of the universal prayer, with much pomp and ritual, the Orthodox patriarch moved from the altar at St. Peter's and watched as the pope celebrated the eucharist. They returned before communion to exchange the kiss of peace, but the Orthodox patriarch did not receive communion. Schism prevented the joining in the one eucharistic banquet for all.

Schism is the refusal to submit to the Roman pontiff or to communion with the members of the Church subject to him.

Code of Canon Law # 751

Schism has almost as many reasons for being as sins can be attributed to the human family. Personal dispositions and personality conflicts, with all of the insensitivity associated with a self-serving group or self-concerned individuals, cause schism. Then nationalism, economic and social influences by which one group or individual lords it over another, cause schism. Rivalry of places, disputes over liturgy, problems of discipline, even an ideal purity for the more perfect Church, can cause schism.

Problems about faith do not separate schismatics. Even matters of theology need not separate, but when joined with human motivation, the rupture of charity takes place. Even the more recent overtures between east and west since the Vatican Council have not wiped out the mutual suspicion. The western Church has withdrawn the excommunication of the east and the east has done likewise, but they remain not only separated but genuinely suspicious of each other.[22] If schism is the rupture of charity, only the restoration of charity can overcome the various schisms that persist into the twentieth century.

■ Heresy ■

Heresy means false teaching or doctrine. Historically, heresies evolved into groups that share much with the larger body but differ with regard to certain beliefs. Historically, this also involved disobedience to authority, or insubordination. Even the terrible inquisition functioned under the guise of persecuting all those who did not believe properly and submit to the authority of the Church.

Many definitions or descriptions of heresy have flourished in history. For some, very simply, to be a heretic means to deny what is fundamental to faith. In a refined vein, heresy is subscribing to a teaching that opposes immediately and directly the truth revealed by God, which contradicts such a teaching. Moreover, this truth must be further authentically proposed by the Church. All of the elements are necessary for true heresy.

> Heresy is the obstinate postbaptismal denial of some truth which must be believed with divine and Catholic faith, or it is likewise an obstinate doubt concerning the same.
>
> *Code of Canon Law #751*

Motivation also figures as part of the understanding of heresy. Attachment to one's opinion in the face of the Church community with contumacy, the refusal to submit to the Church, results in true heresy. The heretic must not only be knowledgeable but also sufficiently obstinate to separate himself or herself from the community.[23]

■ The Causes of Heresy ■

The causes of heresy are the same as the causes of schism with the additional element of understanding faith. Nationalism, economic and social conditions, disputes on discipline and Church practice, can all contribute to the disagreements in theology and then of faith.

■ Various Heresies ■

In early Christianity the heresies developed over the truth of God and the relationship of Jesus to God and the Holy Spirit to each other. Grace and the relationship of God to the human family also spawned heresies. At the time of the reformation, problems of ministry, institution and authority lay at the root of the heresies of Protestantism.

The Anglican community stands apart from the general reform traditions. The heresy did not develop on the basis of discussions of doctrine such as Lutheranism and Calvinism, but on authority and Church practice. Even today many Anglicans refer to themselves as Anglican Catholic in distinction from Roman Catholic.

Heresies have their value. For Augustine they were the occasion to search more profoundly, to make more precise and to clarify the truth. Of necessity they exist and often reveal the ambiguity of formulas in any attempt for faith to seek understanding. They have always been in the Church and will always remain in history.

For centuries the Roman Church dismissed both schismatics and heretics. They did not belong. Since the Vatican Council, those baptized and born into schismatic churches and heretical churches are referred to as members of the Church but not in full communion.[24] Prior to this council the Roman Catholic Church would not even refer to these groups as churches, since only one Church existed as the true Church and that was the Catholic Church and all who were subject to it.

■ Heresies Today ■

After more than four hundred years the differences in doctrine have lessened. Theological disputes mean little to the ordinary Christian, whether Protestant or Catholic. Church practice and Church authority, however, do matter. In this century the ecumenical movement began with great support coming from the United States. Various dialogues continue discussions on doctrine and raise matters of Church practice. The progress made in the last thirty years offers hope for greater progress in the next thirty years.

Both schism and heresy will probably exist forever. With mutual good will on all parts some of the divisions can be overcome. The differences even within Church practice need not destroy the faith and love that remain the hallmark of the Christianity. No matter on what side one finds oneself, the separation is not good, and all efforts to lessen its power merit dedication and commitment.

The Church remains one because of the gift of God, Father, Son and Holy Spirit. The unity of faith and sacraments and a common social life contribute to this unity. The diversity also remains. Unity can be perfected through multiplicity, but also unity can suffer when the multiplicity is not integrated. What the Church has been the Church will be, just as what the Church will be the Church possesses now, even if imperfectly. All the divisions never destroy the fundamental unity of the Church of Jesus Christ.[25]

Study Questions

1. Is the Church really one? Explain.
2. Unity in multiplicity is a philosophical concept. Does this help in understanding how the Church is one?
3. The unity of the Church must relate to the Trinity. Explain.
4. A unity of faith must be the basis in Christianity. How does this remain in spite of the differences in theology?
5. A unity in worship should characterize Christianity? How is this true even in the Catholic Church where there are many rites?
6. Baptism unites all Christians. How is this important for ecumenism ?
7. The Eucharist can unite and can divide. Explain.
8. Social life is important for everyone. How can the Church promote a unity in social life?
9. How can the Church remain one and yet be multiple?
10. What does schism mean to you?
11. Is heresy an idea left over from a previous age? Does it mean anything today? If so, why?
12. What is the value and meaning of ecumenism?

Notes

1. Cf. *The Teaching of the Catholic Church,* edited by K. Rahner (New York: Alba House, 1966), 424–425.

2. *The Evanston Report,* 1955.

3. Cf. Karl Rahner, "The Theology of the Symbol," *Theological Investigations* (Baltimore: Helicon, 1966), 21–244. Rahner not only explains the philosophical relationship between unity and multiplicity but also uses these concepts in his efforts to explain unity and multiplicity in God.

4. Cf. Y. Congar, *L'Eglise une, sainte, catholique et apostolique* (Paris: du Cerf, 1970).

5. "Ecclesia est coetus hominum viatorum eiusdem fidei christianae professionis et eorumdem sacramentorum participatione adunatus sub regime legitimorum pastorum ac praecipue Romani Pontificis" (*Contra.*, lib. III: *De Ecclesia militante*, c. 2). In a similar fashion he writes: "Ecclesia est quaedam convocatio et congregatio hominum baptizatorum, qui eamdem fidem et legem Christi sub Romani Pontificis obedientia profitentur." "The Church is a certain convocation and congregation of baptized people who profess the same faith and law of Christ under the obedience to the Roman Pontiff" (*Christianae doctrinae latior explicatio*, 57).

6. Cf. Congar, 22–28.

7. A full presentation of these individuals can be found in R. Collins, "Representative Figures in the Fourth Gospel," *Downside Review,* Vol. 94 (1976), 26–46, 118–132.

8. Ibid.

9. Cf. J. O'Grady, "The Good Shepherd and the Vine and the Branches," *Biblical Theology Bulletin,* Vol. 8 (1978), 86–89.

10. Cf. O'Grady, *Pillars...,* 16–25.

11. Ibid., 135–143.

12. Ibid., 29–38.

13. Cf. J. Sudbrack, "Prayer," *Sacramentum Mundi,* 74–81.

14. Sometimes the frequent praying of the Lord's prayer brings familiarity. Praying the petitions from the end, backward often helps people to appreciate its meaning:

> God preserve me from the evil that surrounds me and that I so often find within me; do not let me get in over my head in my life for I am always fragile. I want to forgive all those who have offended me, for surely I am in need of being forgiven of all that I have done to others. Help me each day, providing for me all that I need just to

live. I pray that all will recognize your presence on earth
and respond to your call, for you are the holy one of all
and you I call "Abba" as Jesus did.

15. For general ideas on baptism and the eucharist, consult
any standard theological dictionary, e.g., B. Neunheuser, "Baptism," *Sacramentum...*

16. Ibid. Also cf. Congar, 31–38.

17. Some scholars question whether the "breaking of the
bread" in Acts 2:46 and 20:7 is eucharistic. It more clearly seems to
be in Acts 2:42. I am inclined to think that all these refer to the
eucharist.

18. Cf. Congar, 39–46.

19. Each characteristic of the Church interacts and fulfills each
other.These same characteristics will influence Church ministry. The
Church as a communion will be discussed further under the mission
of the Church. This also influences the Church as apostolic.

20. The Vatican Council paid special attention to the unity in
diversity. Cf. *Lumen Gentium,* nn. 6–7. The *Catechism* also refers to
the unity in diversity. "From the beginning this one Church has
been marked by a great diversity which comes from both the variety
of God's gifts and the diversity of those who receive them" (814).

21. Cf. K. Rahner, *On Heresy* (New York: Herder and Herder,
1964); J. Villiger, "Schism," *Sacramentum...*, 6–19.

22. The mutual excommunication was lifted on December 7
1965 when the American cardinal Lawrence Sheehan traveled to
Istanbul to meet with Athenagoras I.

23. Possibly more schismatics and heretics exist in the Church
today than ordinarily recognized. Since most are not sufficiently
knowledgeable and do not have contumacy, they are in fact material
heretics. They live as members of the Church publicly and live in
communion with the Church. These heretics and possibly schismatics live both on the left and on the right. A conservative is not more
secure in avoiding heresy and maintaining charity than the liberal.

24. Cf. *Decree on Ecumenism*, nn. 3–4.

25. Many might consider treating the ecumenical movement
here under unity. I have chosen to treat it under catholicity. Either
place would be appropriate. Placing it under catholicity, in my opinion, safeguards any attempt to denigrate the diversity already
within Christianity from its origins.

7.

The Church Is Holy

Holy, holy, holy, Lord God almighty
Early in the morning our song shall rise to thee
Holy, holy, holy, merciful and mighty
…
God in three persons, blessed trinity.
Holy, holy holy, Lord
God of power and might

Holy, holy, holy is the Lord of hosts.
The whole earth is full of his glory. (Is 6:3)

*G*od alone is holy. The Hebrew word *kadosh* means either to cut off, to separate, or to be bright and shine. Both theories of meaning have proponents, but the more fundamental meaning seems to imply to separate.[1] God is cut off from or separated from all that is not God. Holiness undergirds and pervades all religion. Holiness is not just one attribute among others with God but the attribute that expresses the innermost reality to which all others must relate. By definition even the one who experiences the holy knows there is something more. Holiness is ineffable even while it has its noetic content.[2]

Common to all efforts to explain or describe the holy is an undefined energy, a sense of the numinous, of the imponderable along with the feeling of human inadequacy. When Moses came into contact with God both at the burning bush and on Sinai, he experienced the classic moment of contact with the sacred. He was fascinated and afraid, he experienced the *mysterium tremens* and *mysterium fascinans*.[3]

■ Holiness in the Old Testament ■

In the Old Testament,[4] holiness is related to creation and history, to human experience and conduct, and in particular to election and covenant. Holiness involves the psychological as well as the physical and spiritual aspect of an individual life, as well as the destiny of the community or even the nation. The presence of the holy demands adoration, worship and obedience. In the many encounters with holiness, people encounter wonder and mystery.

Holiness does not belong inherently to creation. God alone is holy, but God has also declared creation to be holy and has made creation holy. The land is holy (Gen 28:16–18; Ex 3:5), the city of Jerusalem is holy (Ps 43:3), and the temple is holy (Ps 5:8; 11:4; 28:2). God is the source of holiness for creation, for the city and for the temple, but God's people must maintain this holiness. When people sin, God and the holy name become desecrated.

HOLY

God
Creation
The land
The temple
People, especially when they worship
The commandments
Priests
The firstborn
Nazarites and all especially dedicated to God
Prophets

God's people are holy when they observe the commandments, which in themselves are holy (Ps 105:42; Jer 23:9). But it is especially when the people join in worship that they become holy (Ex 12:16; Lev 23:27). Above the general population, the priests are called to holiness, with the high priest alone called to enter into the holy of holies and perform the rituals. Ordinary priests officiate in the court at the altar outside the sanctuary and enter the sanctuary only to aid the high priest.

Lay people have another degree of holiness achieved through obedience, especially to the law. God called them from Egypt to make them a special people, and they have an obligation to be holy as God is holy (Lev 11:44–45; 19:2; 20:7–8, 24–26; 22:13–33; Num 15:40; Ex 31:13; Ez 20:12).

Certain individuals among the people are considered holy by status. The first born is always holy; levites are holy (2 Chr 23:6). Those who dedicated themselves to God in a special way, such as the Nazirites, are also holy. Prophets are sometimes considered holy. Elisha is a holy man of God (2 Kgs 4:9) and Jeremiah is set aside from the moment of his conception (Jer 1:5).

Creation, the land, the city and temple, and the commandments are all holy because God so declared. People in particular are holy when they assemble in worship and observe the law. But all holiness rests on the holiness of God. Apart from God, holiness does not exist.

■ Holiness in the New Testament[5] ■

The New Testament continues the traditions of holiness from the Old Testament with an emphasis on the prevailing cultic usage. But what distinguished the New Testament understanding of holy is the association with the Spirit of God. The words *Holy Spirit* occur only three times in the Old Testament (Ps 51:13; Is 63:10–11), while the New Testament uses the expression more than ninety times.

Like the Old Testament, the New Testament affirms that God is holy, but it does so very seldom. Matthew and Luke, in the Our Father, begin with the first petition for the holy name. Revelation refers to God as holy (Rev 16:5). 1 Peter also uses the term: "As he who called you is holy, be holy yourselves in all your conduct" (1 Pet 1:15). In the fourth gospel, Jesus prays to God who is holy (Jn 17:11) and prays that his followers be holy as he is holy (Jn 17:17–19).

The New Testament also presents Jesus as holy, but the attribution is also relatively rare (Mk 1:24; Lk 1:35; 4:34). References to the Spirit as holy help situate the use of the attribute to Jesus. As the holy one, Jesus figures essentially as messiah. As God's holy one, Jesus will deliver the people and redeem them as the suffering servant of God. So in Acts he can be called the holy and righteous one (Acts 3:14).

HOLY

God the Father
Jesus the Son
The Spirit
People: Jews and Gentiles

Hebrews did not use the attribute directly but rather talks about the sanctifying power of Jesus both as priest and as offering. "We have been sanctified through the offering of the body of Jesus Christ once for all" (Heb 10:10; 13:12–13).

Also in the New Testament the people are a holy temple (Eph 2:21; 1 Cor 3:16–17). They are saints (1 Cor 16:1; Rom 15:25–26,31). As the new people of God they are holy especially in their worship. The Church became heir to the holy writings of Israel, the new creation through water and the Holy Spirit, the new heart given life through the Holy Spirit. The holy presence of God in the Old Testament is now made manifest in the people who have been sanctified by the Holy Spirit. The remembering, celebrating, teaching, sacrificing and confessing activities of the holy people, with all of its cultic ritual and worship, takes place in the local church made up of the household of saints.

The idea of a holy people from the Old Testament perpetuated itself in early Christian worship (Heb 9:15–22; 12:18–24; 1 Pet 1:14–16; 2:9–10; Eph 2:12–18). Both Jews and Gentiles are now reconciled with each other and with God, so they together become the holy temple to the Lord (Eph 2:16). Called to be holy (Rom 1:7; 1 Cor 1:2), they live a new life based on the presence of the Holy Spirit within.

The authors of Ephesians and Colossians[6] both describe the life of the holy ones in the Church. They must live a new life that flows from what they have become. Living a moral life does not bring holiness, but holiness demands living a moral life. The beginnings of the holy life can be traced to baptism. It reaches its fulfillment in the eschatological kingdom.

Throughout the Bible, the many references to holiness join God to people in the Old Testament as well as the New Testament. The very essence of God has become part of human history. Creation is holy, but especially people, and in particular those who have been sanctified by Jesus through the Holy Spirit.

■ The Church Is Holy ■

God is holy, Jesus is holy, the Spirit is holy, creation is holy and the people are holy, especially when they worship, but is the Church holy? If the Church is fundamentally the people of God, then the Church is sinful and holy inasmuch as people are both, but can the Church be considered holy apart from the holiness of its members?

If God is holy and if God has made both Israel and the followers of Jesus holy, even though a dialectic exists between what is offered and what is accepted, then the Church is holy by the offering. The Church already expresses the holy reign of God even if it is not yet the complete and holy reign of God apart from its members. The Church is its members and more than its members. God called the Church as an assembly, as a gathering, as an institution to holiness, and so the Church is holy through the gift of God.

Jesus lived and died as the sign of salvation to the nations, the sign of the holy presence of God in human history. When Jesus chose to perpetuate this sign in all of human history through the Church, then the Church takes on some of the holiness of Jesus. The holy Church makes salvation and God visible. The holiness of Jesus continues in the Church.

THE CHURCH IS HOLY

Makes the saving presence of God visible
Manifests the holiness of Jesus
The Holy Spirit is the soul of the Church
The sacraments are holy
People are saints

The Holy Spirit is the soul of the Church. The acts of the Church in its sacraments are effected through the power of the Holy Spirit, and so the Spirit also makes the Church holy. The activities of the Church, in all that it does, express and present the power of the Spirit. People and even things become holy because of the Spirit in the Church.

Father, Son and Holy Spirit make the one Church a holy Church. The gift of God the Father and the ministry given by the Son and accomplished through the Spirit invest the church with an inherent holiness. The very nature of the Church, the meaning of the Church, involves holiness. Throughout the past two thousand years, the holy Church has manifested the holiness of God by continuing the ministry of Jesus to all people through the power of the Spirit of God. The Church is holy.

■ Sin and the Holy Church ■

Historically, theologians have struggled with sin in the Church. Some stated that the Church is not without sinners but is without sin.[7] That seems too objectified, but it remains sufficient for many. The fathers of the Church wrote of the long line of sinners in salvation history—Rahab, Tamar, Magdalene—and used these figures (all women) as images of the Church: sinful but beloved of God. Others say that the Church is holy because it is becoming less sinful or that the Church will be holy in the future when in the eschatological kingdom of God the Church will be perfect, pure, sinless and stainless.

No doubt the Church is sinful because its members are sinful but is that all? Does sin actually affect the very structure and nature of the Church just as holiness permeates the very structure and nature of the Church?

Throughout the centuries Christians have continually attempted to return to the truly "holy" Church. Spiritualists have punctuated Church history at regular intervals. Tertullian declared that the Church of his day was not the true Church of the Spirit because it did not cast out adulterers. Since then Christianity has seen Montanists, Novatians, Donatists, Cathari, Albigensians, even the Spiritualists of the Franciscan tradition, Hussites and the reformers of the sixteenth century, all calling for the truly holy Church to arise from the sin and corruption of the present Church.

PURISTS

Montanists	Moravians
Novatians	Methodism of Whitefield
Donatists	Quakers
Cathari	Pietists
Albigensians	Jansenists
Hussites	Quietists

Many of the accusations by all such reformers need attention. For the most part, the accusations were true. Sin and evil and corruption did exist in the Church of their time. The same can be said for the Church today. Such attacks are just precisely because the Church proclaims salvation, preaches in the name of the one holy God, dispenses grace through its sacramental system, and believes that it must convert and save everyone and yet seems to measure itself with a double standard.

■ Holiness and Sin: Constitutive of the Church ■

A possible way out of the morass of sin and corruption is admitting that such evil is constitutive of the Church itself, even as holiness is constitutive. Sinners belong in the Church and form the building blocks of the holy temple. This does not refer to the person who fails in telling the truth, or the adulterer or the uncharitable person, but rather the one who truly lacks the fullness of God's grace. That is every believer. Such a person functions not just as a peripheral member but as an actual building block of the holy temple of God. All fall short. All lack the fullness of grace. All are constitutively sinners even as each is the embodiment in a personal way of the grace of God in the world.[8]

Only on the shores of eternity will the angels sort out the good fish and the bad (Mt 13:47–50). The tares grow among the wheat both in the sanctuary and in the body of the Church with little distinction. Such teaching, moreover, does not imply that these people really do not belong. They do. They are part of the Church that manifests divine salvation.

The Church may possess the Holy Spirit but never in the fullest sense. The Church may possess God's saving grace but never in a complete sense. The Church may offer salvation through its members but that salvation is fully realized only in the experience of eternal life, begun here but perfected through death.

To say that there are sinners in the Church does not respond to the issue. Sinners are members, intimates, part of the manifestation of the saving presence of God in human history. If everyone is a sinner, according to Paul (Rom 1–3) and yet these sinners remain members of the Church, then the Church must necessarily be sinful.[9] "This is a truth of faith, not an elementary fact of experience, and it is a shattering truth."[10]

■ Sin in the Church ■

The study of those most responsible for the Church also manifests the sinfulness of the Church. When ecclesiastics do sin, in their private lives, it affects their public life as leaders of the Church. As sinners, the sinful condition certainly influences "very substantially their concrete mode of action as official representatives of the Church."[11] The Church then can be sinful in its very actions. Certainly this activity goes against the presence of the Spirit, but a sinful Church has no other possibility.

Several consequences flow from the acceptance of the Church

as sinful even while it remains always the holy Church. Certainly the Church can never look down on human institutions with a sense of arrogance. All human structures and organizations are flawed, as is the Church. In fact the sinfulness of the Church is far worse than the sinfulness of other human institutions. The Church by its mission manifests the truth, the goodness, the love and beauty of God to all people. Sin mars this mission and compromises the holiness.

A sinful Church also fails terribly with regard to its own members. Throughout its history, the Church has persecuted, humiliated, estranged, cast out and alienated its members officially. Even those later judged as holy, as saints, have suffered precisely because of the sinful nature of the Church. The sin and evil that must of necessity exist within the body of Christ cannot be directed only to those who have a particular interest in evil and sin, but almost especially to those whom God seems to love in a special way. Saints were not always saints, and saints have their fair share of misunderstanding and even persecution. "A prophet is not without honor except in his own country and in his own house" (Mt 13:57).

■ Church Scandals ■

But how do members come to grips with this sinfulness? To try to appeal to an ideal Church does not work. Only one Church exists, and it is a Church filled with scandal on every level. To try to separate the divine from the human and vice versa is impossible. The divine finds practical and experiential expression in the human, and the human remains sinful.

Some have tried to cover up the scandals and the sins. That also does not work. Rather, honesty demands an appraisal based on history and not on hopeful fantasy of what might have been. The dark patch in the history of the Church remains dark with no whitewashing. Failure, corruption, misuse of power, underhanded dealings, sexual sins and scandals are part of the history because the Church is sinful constitutively. The sins of the members are the sins of the Church, whether clergy or religious or lay. Denial only makes matters worse.

■ Holiness in the Midst of Sin ■

Recognizing the sinfulness makes it possible to see the holiness and the honor and the glory. To weep over personal sins and the sins of the whole Church brings an awareness of the true holiness that comes only from God as a gift and not as something merited or deserved. The Church has generously bestowed on human history manifold graces from the one loving God. The Church has also sinned grievously in human history. The one who knows the sin will also be able to profess belief in the holy Church. The truly humble Church stands guilty before Jesus.

Jesus had made himself holy so that his followers might be holy (Jn 17:19). He knows the sins of this holy Church better than anyone. Yet like the woman taken in adultery:

> And at the end the Lord will be alone with the woman And then he will stand erect and look upon this prostitute, his bride, and ask her, "Woman, where are your accusers? Has no one condemned you?" And she will answer with inexpressible repentance and humility, "No one, Lord." But the Lord will come close to her and say, "Then neither shall I condemn you." He will kiss her forehead and murmur, "My bride, my Holy Church."[12]

Study Questions

1. What does holy mean to you?
2. God alone is holy. How can people be holy?
3. Do you think the Church is holy? Why?
4. Do you think the Church is sinful? Why?
5. How can the Church be both constitutively holy and constitutively sinful?
6. Is it too strong a statement to assert that the Church is constitutively sinful?
7. Sinners belong in the Church. What implications can be taken from this statement?
8. If the Church has actually sinned against some of its members, does this give people reason to abandon the Church?
9. What is attractive about a sinful but holy Church?
10. How do you react to the recent scandals in the Church?

Notes

1. Any standard dictionary of the Bible will give a fuller explanation of "holy." See R. Hodgson, "Holiness," *The Anchor Bible Dictionary*, 237–254.

2. Cf. R. Otto, *The Idea of the Holy* (New York: Oxford University Press, 1958); William James, *The Varieties of Religious Experience* (New York: Random House, 1929).

3. Cf. Otto and James. Otto offers the classic understanding of the "numinous." James presents four characteristics of religious experience: ineffable, noetic content, transient and the person is passive. See James, Lectures 16 and 17.

4. Hodgson offers a good summary of the meaning in the Old Testament. Cf. "Holiness," 237–248.

5. Ibid., 249–254.

6. Cf. Brown, *The Churches...*, chapter 3.

7. Such is the classic opinion. Cf. C. Journet, *L'Eglise du Verbe Incarne* (Paris: du Cerf, 1951), 904.

8. "Christ, holy and innocent and undefiled, knew nothing of sin but came only to expiate the sins of the people. The Church, however, clasping sinners to her bosom, at once holy and always in need of purification, follows constantly the path of penance and renewal" (*Lumen Gentium,* 8). "All members of the Church, including her ministers, must acknowledge they are sinners. In everyone, the weeds of sin will still be mixed with the good wheat of the Gospel until the end of time. Hence the Church gathers sinners already caught up in Christ's salvation but still on the way to holiness" (*Catechism,* 827).

9. Cf. Karl Rahner, "The Church of Sinners," *Theological Investigations,* Vol. VI (Baltimore: Helicon, 1969), 260.

10. Ibid.

11. Ibid.

12. Ibid., 269.

8.

The Church Is Catholic

"Catholic," in most people's minds, has come to mean the Christian Church that has allegiance to the bishop of Rome. Even more specifically, the word denotes the group of Christians that distinguish themselves, and are distinguished, from Protestant, Anglican and Orthodox Churches. In most instances people need not even add the adjective *Roman* to Catholic, because for most people Roman Catholic is the same as Catholic.[1]

The word comes from two Greek words, *kath,* a preposition meaning "according to," and *olos,* meaning "whole, entire" or "complete." The word may also mean "according to the assembly," or, in a general and then in a derived way, "universal." The word does not appear in the New Testament applied to the Church. One time it appears as an adverb in Acts 4:18 meaning "at all."

■ Catholic in the Early Church Fathers ■

The first use of the word occurs in the letter of Ignatius of Antioch to Smyrna (dated c. 110): "Where the bishop is, there is also the community; the same that where there is Christ Jesus, the Church is catholic" (8,1). The exact interpretation of the words of Ignatius has a long history. For some, Ignatius refers to a parallel between the local church, with the bishop presiding, and the Catholic Church where Christ is the head. For others, the saying means that the authentic Church is where the bishop presides, for the bishop mirrors Christ.[2]

Actually, both interpretations seem necessary. Later, in *The Martyrdom of Polycarp, catholic* means both universal and true. Clement of Alexandria uses the term to mean the true Church, as does Tertullian. *The Muratorian Fragment* employs the expression to dis-

122

tinguish the authentic Church from Christian sects. By the beginning
of the third century, for many, the sense has been fully established,
meaning the true Church throughout the world in which each local
community finds itself in communion with the universal Church.[3]

THE MARTYRDOM OF POLYCARP (155–157)

The Church of God which sojourns in Smyrna... to all the dioceses
of the holy and catholic Church (1,1).

...the whole Catholic Church throughout the world (8.1).

...the wonderful martyr Polycarp, who in our days was an apostolic
and prophetic teacher, bishop of the Catholic Church in Smyrna
(16,2).

■ Catholic in the Fourth Century ■

In Christian creeds and baptismal formulae, the word appears
early. Throughout the fourth century *catholic* is used in the baptismal creed of Egypt, the creed of Cyril of Jerusalem, that of Saint
Epiphanius, and in Nicea.

ST. CYRIL OF JERUSALEM (350)

(The Church is called) Catholic because it extends over the whole
world from end to end of the earth; it teaches universally and infallibly all the doctrines that ought to come to human knowledge, concerning things visible and invisible, heavenly and earthly, and
because it brings every race of men into subjection to godliness,
governors and governed, learned and unlearned; and because it
universally treats and heals every class of sins, those committed with
the soul and those with the body; and it possesses within itself every
conceivable form of virtue in deeds and in words and in the spiritual
gifts of every description *(Catechetical Lectures 18, 23).*

Augustine likes the notion of geographically universal.
Catholic means the Church spread throughout the world. During
this period the Catholic Church is the Church opposed to heretical
groups and not just sectarian groups.[4]

■ Catholic in the Middle Ages ■

In the middle ages, Albert the Great added a quantitative dimension to these notions of geography and authenticity. Christ offers the fullness of bread and of life. This the Church communicates through faith and the sacraments. The presence of faith expressed throughout the known world makes the Church *catholic*.[5]

In later centuries, catholic truths were those necessary for salvation.[6] In the Catholic Church one finds the totality of the sacred and all that is necessary to experience the saving presence of God through Jesus. In the Church, redemption and grace become effective. People experience Christian redemption and salvation made possible through Jesus by his death and resurrection and now made operative and accessible through the Church.

After the division between eastern and western churches in 1054, the churches of the east became known as the *Orthodox* churches, to describe those Christian churches that remained faithful to the councils of Ephesus and Chalcedon. The western churches living in communion with the patriarch of the west, the pope, became known as the Catholic Church.[7]

■ The Protestant Period ■

During the Protestant period polemics became narrow and apologetical. The Catholic Church was the true Church defending itself against the reformers. The sense of the geographical, however, continued with the sending out of missionaries and the exploration of non-European lands. The apologetical tone lasted into the twentieth century. Only with the reforms advocated by the Second Vatican Council did the word *catholic* move away from a narrow and apologetical meaning.[8]

During the period of the reformation, the word *Roman* was added to Catholic to emphasize the connection to Rome. Officially, however, the Church of Rome continues to use only *Catholic*. The Catholic Church has always included more than the Roman Church.[9]

Today for many people the word connotes diversity and universality when used with the small *c* and Roman Catholic when used with a large *C*. Such change in usage might appear helpful to some, but then the word loses its theological meaning. The Christian and Roman Church understanding of itself as *Catholic* has roots in the Christian understanding of God.

■ Theology of Catholicity[10] ■

Theology studies God. If a theology of being *Catholic* exists, then this must have something to do with the study of God. But since all theology is a human effort to understand faith, a source from above must be joined to a source from below. The Trinity and the human family create the foundation for being Catholic.

■ Universal Salvation ■

God wills the unity of all peoples accomplished through the acceptance of divine salvation. Certainly such a divine will must also take into consideration human freedom, but the ultimate will of God with regard to the salvation of the human race is assured, even if this cannot be predicated equivocally to each individual. God has decreed salvation for all.

The universal means of salvation, in spite of all the evil and sin, is Jesus Christ. In the same way that God the Father sent the Son to be the savior of the world, God has willed that the Church continue this mission to all peoples. The Church has become the universal sign of salvation to the nations as was Jesus in his ministry.

This call for universal salvation, however, is made in a human fashion. Grace rests and builds upon nature. When humanity has achieved the fullness of salvation, even the cosmos will be affected (Rom 8:19–23). Throughout the New Testament the fullness and universality of salvation forms a recurring theme. God calls all people to salvation, and the universe also shares in this saving presence of God.

> He is the head of the body, the Church; he is the beginning, the firstborn from the dead, that in everything he might be preeminent. For in him all the fullness of God was pleased to dwell and through him to reconcile to himself all things, whether on earth or in heaven, making peace by the blood of his cross. (Col 1:18–20)

> For he has made known to us in all wisdom and insight the mystery of his will, according to his purpose which he set forth in Christ, as a plan for the fullness of time, to unite all things in him, things in heaven and things on earth. (Eph 1:9–10)

Jesus makes the reign of God, present here on earth on a universal plane with cosmic proportion. The Church continues this mission and participates in the actual building of the reign of God, first spiritually, and then ultimately this will involve the entire universe.

The Spirit accomplishes in the Church what Jesus began in his ministry. The Holy Spirit has become the source of catholicity, accomplishing a communion among all peoples. The Church under the guidance of the Spirit has reached out to all who will listen and has offered the saving presence of God to all peoples of all times and places. No one is excluded, no culture neglected, no tradition abandoned, but all have been subsumed into the power of the Spirit in the Church.

■ The One Universe ■

The catholicity from above through the Trinity finds its human expression below. The human family is one in spite of the varied cultures, races, languages, traditions, hopes and expectations. The fullness of Christ brings this diversity into a unity that is at the same time universal. A common humanity forms the basis for a universal Church. Differences need not lessen but can enrich this common bond.

In recent years the human race has become more conscious of the cosmos with the exploration of space. What the human race does here on earth has its effect on the universe, just as the universe has its effect on this small planet. Christianity has long professed an interrelatedness between earth and universe under the one creator God.

Even the possibility of other life forms does not destroy the universality of God and the universality of salvation. God offers a saving presence to all in the universe, and all and everything in the universe are included. The restoration of all things in God, with peace and love and justice and liberty for all, has begun in Jesus and extends outward to include all people and all creation. The Spirit continues this restoration, and individuals contribute and accept the effects of this divine will and plan.

■ Humanity and History ■

Humanity lives in history. The human race lives dynamically with an ever more powerful impulse for full development and realization. This means that no one period of history can claim a perfection in salvation or a completion of God's plan. History demands an ongoing process in which the will of God is realized. As humanity changes and advances, or even declines, the saving power of God continues in the Church. The change is good and necessary. What humanity has become needs to be integrated into all that humanity has already been. Only then can the dynamism of the human race continue toward its fulfillment in God.

Catholicity belongs to the universal Church as an attribute and as a responsibility.

> So it is that this messianic people, although it does not actually include all people, and may more than once look like a small flock, is nonetheless a lasting and sure seed of unity, hope and salvation for the whole human race. Established by Christ as a fellowship of life, charity, and truth, it is also used by him as an instrument of the redemption of all, and is sent forth into the whole world as the light of the world and the salt of the earth.[11]

The entire Church has this obligation to be catholic as does the local church and even individual believers. This catholicity presupposes a profound communion uniting individuals to the local community and then being in turn united to the universal Church. This universality will distinguish the Church from any Christian sect. The latter avoids inclusivity and causes a separation instead of a universal unity.

■ Quantitative and Qualitative Catholicity   ■

Quantitative catholicity also always includes qualitative catholicity. Since the universal Church rests upon the universality of humanity and the universality of God's will for salvation, the qualitative universality must include the quantitatively universality. Both are tasks to be accomplished through the Spirit and are not yet realized.

In *Lumen Gentium* 13, dedicated to catholicity, the fathers of the council declared that the people of God are to be found in all places and among all peoples. Since the reign of God is not of this world, the Church takes away nothing from the temporal order. Rather, insofar as they are good, the Church takes to itself "the ability, resources and customs of all people." Catholicity demands the incorporation into the Church of the gifts of diverse cultures, races, and nationalities. No one is excluded, since all belong by the universal decree of salvation for all.[12]

■ The Universal Church ■

Being Catholic also means having a sense of the universal Church. The Church is not just the local community or a sum of all the local communities throughout the world. Nor can it ever be, however, a monolithic institution spreading out from Rome as many tentacles from the head of the octopus. Being catholic means a fullness as well as the communion of churches.

The Church on earth also includes both saints and sinners, for it is also the holy and sinful Church. The universality of the Church, its catholicity, means that it includes just and unjust, rich and poor; in fact, all of humanity finds representation within its arms. *Catholic* means a world Church including more than just western civilization.[13]

The catholicity of the Church also transcends time. Both the baptized on earth and those faithful departed are part of the Catholic Church. The belief in the communion of saints presumes some fellowship with those who have died in the Lord. Catholics can feel comfortable with praying to and for those who have preceded them in faith, for all are part of the one Catholic Church, both the living and the dead.

■ Catholicity and Truth ■

Being Catholic also has meant that the Church is open to all truth wherever found. No single doctrine, ritual, creed, text or interpretation of scripture expresses fully the catholicity of the Church. Nor can any one theology. Catholicity includes a broad spectrum of theologies, spiritualities, and concrete expressions of Christian life. Whatever is truly human and good can find a place and an embrace within the Catholic Church.

■ Ecumenism[14] ■

No discussion about catholicity can exclude the ecumenical movement, the activity on the part of many to restore Christian unity. At the beginning of this century,[15] many Christians, pained by the separation within Christianity, began a grassroots movement for unity. Slowly, with much pain and great effort, the seeds planted so many years ago began to sprout in various places around the world. At first cautious, the Roman Church embraced ecumenism more fully at the Second Vatican Council.[16] John XXIII not only set the ecumenical tone for the council but also established the Secretariat for Christian Unity.[17]

Acknowledging the unity of faith and baptism, the council nevertheless recognized the problems inherent in a separated Christianity.

> The division among Christians impede the Church from effecting the fullness of catholicity proper to her in those of her sons who, though joined to her by baptism, are yet separated from full communion. Furthermore, the Church herself finds it more difficulty to express in actual life here full catholicity in all its aspects.[18]

The council makes clear that the Church has not lost its catholicity but realizes that it is yet to be fully attained. Only through the mutual efforts to understand, to work together and to pray together can the various Christian churches fulfill the call to catholicity.

■ Promoting Christian Unity ■

If the Church is catholic, then every effort should be made to promote Christian unity. The Roman Church[19] may not and should not denigrate the various other Christian churches for their lack of catholicity, since no one Christian Church has yet fulfilled the obligations of this attribute.[20] The Orthodox Church may in some ways make a greater contribution to catholicity than the Protestant denominations. Nevertheless, each Christian Church, through its efforts to achieve the salvation of God for all, expresses catholicity.

The principle of loyalty to the different traditions forms the foundation for all ecumenical dialogue. Friendship can easily develop from a common faith and common baptism. Concern for the spiritual welfare of all Christians, an awareness and knowledge of the various Christian traditions, and a willingness to learn from each tradition should characterize ecumenical dialogue. Prayer in common facilitates this fellowship even if full intercommunion is not yet officially possible.[21]

If the attribute "catholic" depends upon the Trinity and the good will of all Christians, then the success of the ecumenical movement can be assured. As with all of the attributes of the Church, catholicity must never be seen as a perfection accomplished but as a task to be realized.

Study Questions

1. What does "catholic" mean to you?

2. "Catholic" usually means Roman Catholic to most people. Why does the presence of other churches within the Catholic Church help in understanding unity in diversity?

3. Catholicity must relate to the will of God for the salvation of all peoples. Why and how?

4. The one human family forms the basis for the Church as catholic. How does this affect diversity in the Church?

5. Ecumenism can be discussed under the heading of the Church as one or the Church as Catholic. What differences flow from where ecumenism is studied?

6. If you are Roman Catholic, what are you proud of with regard to your Church?

7. If you are Christian but not Roman Catholic, what are you proud of with regard to your church?

8. How can all churches in Christianity be "catholic"?

Notes

1. Actually this is not very accurate. There are twenty-two churches that are Catholic, including the Roman Church. These churches have three things in common: faith, sacraments and submission to the authority of the Bishop of Rome. They have four distinguishing marks: liturgy, theology, spirituality and governance. For more information on the many Catholic churches, see Ronald Beshara, *Being a Maronite Catholic* (Danbury: Diocese of St. Maron, 1989).

2. Cf. Congar, 150–151.

3. Ibid., 151–152.

4. Ibid., 153.

5. Ibid., 157–158.

6. Ibid.

7. Ibid.

8. Ibid., 159.

9. Cf. Beshara.

10. Congar, 161–165 The emphasis on the Trinity comes from the work of Congar.

11. *Lumen Gentium, 9.*

12. A geographical concept does not explain catholicity, nor a numerical concept. Neither cultural diversity nor the oldest church explains catholicity. (Cf. H. Kung, *The Church*, New York: Doubleday, 1967, 388–389.) Catholicity is theological.

13. In the synod meeting in Rome in 1985, 74 percent of the participants came from countries other than Europe and North America.

14. Some may wonder why ecumenism is discussed here rather than under the study of the unity of the Church. Both places are possible. I chose to discuss ecumenism here because it seems to suit better the understanding of "catholicity" even though it also can fit under the unity of the Church. A good presentation of the problems of ecumenism with some suggestions for solutions can be found in H. Fries and K. Rahner, *The Unity of the Churches* (New York: Paulist, 1985). Originally the publication of this work caused little reaction until it was reviewed by D. Ols, O.P., professor of theology at the Angelicum in Rome. Fries and Rahner offer practical solutions to present problems in ecumenism based on eight theses. For a summary of the book and a critique, see "Unity of the Churches: An Ecumenical Controversy," *Theology Digest*, Vol. 33 (1986), 329–332.

15. Many ecumenists will date the modern ecumenical movement to the gathering of chiefly Protestant missionary organizations in 1910 that later developed into two organizations, the "Faith and Order" group and the "Life and Work Group." In 1948 the two joined to form the World Council of Churches.

16. Leo XIII anticipated the desire for Christian unity and set the tone for an official response in his encyclical *Satis Cognitum.* Unity resides in the Catholic Church. Not until Pius XI did another pope express interest in Christian unity. This pontiff wanted better relations with the Orthodox Church and encouraged the Malines Conversations with Anglicans (1921–1926), led by Cardinal Mercier. Under Pius XII the oldest ecumenical dialogue began in France in 1937. In 1948 the Holy Office set down some cautious but encouraging rules for Catholics to participate in ecumenical conversations.

17. Paul VI took the first major steps by applying the principles formulated in the council document to actual ecumenical dialogue. The recent encyclical of John Paul II, *Ut Unum Sint,* has furthered the involvement of the Catholic Church in the ecumenical movement.

18. *Decree on Ecumenism, 4.*

19. In the strictest sense as already noted, the word "Catholic"

does not apply exclusively to the Roman Catholic Church. "Catholic" means more than just Roman and more than just western. This book has centered on the Roman Catholic Church, acknowledging the existence of the many other Catholic churches that are not Roman and yet in full communion with the bishop of Rome.

20. In *Lumen Gentium* the Vatican Council broadened the idea of catholicity to include churches outside the Roman Catholic Church, and in the *Decree on Ecumenism* the council spoke of these churches as possessing varying degrees of catholicity.

21. Eucharistic sharing is practiced on most occasions with no reference to official guidelines. Protestants regularly participate in Roman Catholic eucharists, and many Roman Catholics will accept the eucharist in protestant celebrations, especially on special occasions such as weddings, funerals and the like. Some dioceses have interpreted the guidelines for Protestants to receive the eucharist in the broadest of terms. The three conditions are as follows: being deprived of the service of one's minster, believing in the presence of Jesus in the Eucharist, and the personal need to join in the eucharistic celebration. For some this can be true only in the case of imminent death. For others, these conditions can be verified in ordinary family celebrations such as those enumerated above, and also first communions, confirmations, etc. The *Decree on Ecumenism* states: "As for common worship, however, it may not be regarded as a means to be used indiscriminately for the restoration of unity among Christians. Such worship depends chiefly on two principles: it should signify the unity of the Church; it should provide a sharing in the means of grace. The fact that it should signify unity generally rules out common worship. Yet the gaining of a needed grace sometimes commends it" (n. 8). See also J. Witte, "The Basis of Intercommunion," *Gregorianum*, Vol. 34 (1970), 87–111.

9.

The Church Is Apostolic

*T*he one, holy, and catholic Church is also apostolic, a defining link that binds the present Church to the Church of the apostles:

> You form a building which rises on the foundation of the apostles and prophets, with Christ Jesus himself as the capstone. (Eph 2:20)

An unbroken continuity not only gives assurance of the relationship between the present Church and the early Christian community but also promises a link to the future. The once and future Church are one and the same since all go back to the original followers of Jesus. The Second Vatican Council declares that "the bishops by divine institution have taken the place of the apostles as pastors of the Church."[1] The Church rests upon the apostles. The history of the Church includes some relationship to the earliest followers of the Lord, especially the apostles.

■ The New Testament ■

The gospel of Matthew knew the need for authority and organization. He recognized that the future of the Church depended on the Gentiles rather than the Jewish Christians, and also concluded that the Church will be present in human history for many years to come. In the conclusion of his gospel, he professed a line of authority through the apostles to Jesus.

> And Jesus came and said to them, "All authority in heaven and on earth has been given to me; go therefore and make disciples of all nations, baptizing them in the name of the Father and of the Son and of the Holy Spirit,

133

> teaching them to observe all that I have commanded you.
> And lo, I am with you always to the close of the age."
> (Matt 28:18-20)

In the Acts of the Apostles, Luke also founds the early Church on the relationship to the apostles:

> And they devoted themselves to the apostles' teaching
> and fellowship, to the breaking of bread and the prayers.
> (Acts 2:42)

No one can precisely pinpoint the circumstances that gave rise to this passage from Matthew. The presence of the liturgical formula, with baptism in the name of Father, Son and Holy Spirit, points in itself to the later origin of the saying. The need for an organized Church also supports the view that the passage comes more from the time of Matthew than that of Jesus. The idea behind the passage—the need for succession—probably arose quickly in the early Christian communities. Since each gospel depicts Peter with a specific role and associates him closely with the Lord, the author of Matthew would be very much in conformity with the ministry of Jesus to present Peter in a significant Church role.

Luke in Acts, following his tradition in the gospel, seeks a firm foundation for his Gentile Christian community. Whatever happens in the Church toward the end of the first century rests upon the foundations of the apostles. The Church devoted itself to what the apostles taught, and thus the contemporary church of Luke can feel secure in its traditions. What the Church teaches today can be traced to ministers of the word, to eyewitnesses, the disciples and apostles, and then to Jesus.

CONTINUITY

- God offers revelation to humanity
- Jesus expresses this revelation in his ministry, death and resurrection
- Eyewitnesses proclaim the Jesus tradition to others
- Ministers of the word continue the function of the eyewitnesses
- Individuals write the gospels and epistles and other New Testament writings
- People of all ages can trace their faith to Jesus and to God

---

The New Testament shows that both the twelve and the other apostles figured prominently in the early Church. The two groups however, as previously noted, cannot be used interchangeably. Paul, as we also saw, was clearly an apostle but not one of the twelve. The same can be said for other early followers (2 Cor 8:23; 1 Cor 12:28; Eph 4:11). Some are called apostles, and other instances in the New Testament seem to presume that apostles are more than the twelve.

■ Apostolic Succession[2] ■

The New Testament demonstrates that the apostles in fact had no successors nor did the twelve. Apostolic ministry, however, must and did continue. In fact, the ministry of the Church involves more than just an unbroken chain of authority. The ministry of the Church today involves the spiritual ideal of the disciples and apostles, the dedicated and enthusiastic commitment to preaching embodied in Paul, the virtues of presbyters/bishops, and the sacramental ministry, especially the breaking of bread.[3] The Church maintains apostolic ministry in a most complex way.

In the past, the understanding of apostolic succession as the link between bishop and apostles through the imposition of hands was too narrow. The more recent Lima Document presents apostolic succession in a broader context:

> Apostolic tradition in the Church means continuity in the permanent characteristics of the Church of the apostles: witness to the apostolic faith, proclamation and fresh interpretation of the gospel, celebration of baptism and the eucharist, the transmission of ministerial responsibilities, communion in prayer, love, joy and suffering, service to the sick and needy, unity among the local churches and sharing the gifts which the Lord has given to each.[4]

The above statement can seem too broad especially when compared to the usual understanding of apostolicity in Roman Catholicism. In an ecumenical document, however, such might be expected, especially when the underlying element is the validity of ordination and true succession among the many Christian churches.[5]

The Church needs continuity. No one can doubt that. But precisely how this continuity can be maintained, especially in the light of the two thousand years of history, has various possibilities and proponents. The past often gives guidance for the present. What the earliest Church fathers believed and taught has value for the Church of today.

Irenaeus gives his understanding of apostolicity, which also gives some guidance today.

> True doctrine ought to be found in the tradition received from the apostles by the bishops or the presbyters, instituted by them and transmitted to their successors up to the present time.[6]

Apostolicity involves true teaching. Apostolicity involves the very "roots" of Christianity. If no one can feel comfortable that what is taught and happening in the Church today has some connection to Jesus through apostolic succession, then Christianity becomes completely relativized. Being apostolic avoids this dilemma. Luke himself wanted to avoid this problem and so he wrote both the gospel of Luke and the Acts of the Apostles to respond to this need of his day.

TRUE TEACHING

Jesus
The apostles, including Paul
Presbyters/bishops
The pope with the bishops
All under the guidance of the Holy Spirit

■ Apostolicity ■

The apostolicity of the Church can never be reduced to apostolic succession, however close they may be related. The apostolic college certainly continues in the college of bishops. The early fathers of the Church, Clement, Irenaeus, Tertullian, Cyprian, Hippolytus and others, all relate bishops to the apostles. Today, bishops are the principal teachers of the Church and thus carry on an apostolic ministry. As principal teachers, they offer guidance and direction, especially when they gather as a college such as at the Second Vatican Council. Something similar can be said for the gathering of national conferences of bishops.[7] The question of the relationship between apostles and bishops in the New Testament, however, offers two different approaches and two viewpoints, that of Luke and Paul.[8]

■ Luke and the Apostles ■

Debate continues on the precise relationship between the twelve and apostles in the writings of Luke. Some claim Luke used the title apostles for the twelve exclusively. Others see the title used of the twelve more as primary than exclusive. Further discussion centers on the role of the twelve in the early Church. Certainly Luke does not show them as missionaries, but perhaps for Luke they had a certain power of approving missionary activity.

Also in Luke the twelve are not depicted as bishops. Luke offers no evidence in Acts that any one of the twelve ever presided over a local church.[9] It is also generally agreed that James, the leader of the Jerusalem community, was not called a bishop, and so was not the same person as James, son of Alphaeus, one of the twelve.[10] Peter is sometimes called the bishop of Antioch, but no supporting evidence exists in Acts. Most Roman Catholics would remark that Peter was surely the first bishop of Rome. However, no evidence from history or archeology attests to such a position.[11] Luke does not present the twelve as bishops or local leaders. The apostolate of the twelve and the presbyterate-episcopate existed at the same time but with different functions.

Some will try to relate the function of the twelve to bishops through sacramental powers to baptize, to celebrate the eucharist and to forgive sins. The New Testament offers no evidence for such a handing on. The conclusion from the New Testament seems clear: there were no successors to the twelve. The symbolism of the twelve responsible for the founding of the renewal of Israel was unique.[12]

Yet Luke does have the apostles fulfill distinct roles in the Acts of the Apostles. The problem of the Hellenists in Acts 6:1–6 was far more serious than merely the distribution of goods. The Hellenists were not great supporters of the temple, while many Jewish Christians were. The decision to give the Hellenists their own leaders prepared for the future Gentile Church. The implications were evident when persecution broke out. The Hellenists were scattered, but those loyal to the temple (the apostles? the twelve?) were not. In fact the Hellenists probably became the first missionaries.

The second great decision made by the apostles concerned Jewish law. The conclusion in Acts has already been discussed. Gentiles need not become Jews first and then Christians. The law was no longer binding. Jesus offers a freedom from observance, especially of circumcision and the dietary laws. Even if some Jews wanted to continue to observe these laws when they became Christians, they could not impose them on Gentiles.[13]

THE ROLE OF THE APOSTLES IN LUKE

- Settle matters of concern for the whole Church
- Leadership for the Gentiles
- Relationship of Christianity to Jewish laws

The twelve figured prominently in these two decisions.[14] In Acts 6:2, the twelve call together the multitude and propose a solution. In Acts 15:2–29, the apostles and the presbyters welcome Paul and Barnabas. Luke presents the twelve as a kind of council presiding over matters of consequence for the future of Christianity.

Some, of course, will say that Luke invented the whole scenario. Luke cannot always be trusted as an historian in spite of his protestations that such was what he desired. With the recent discoveries from Qumran,[15] however, it seems plausible that the early Church took over for its own structure the organization of the sectarians at Qumran. Thus Luke presents the twelve, those closest to Jesus, as a kind of council that convoked sessions to deal with major problems. The Lucan apostle, since he was the companion of Jesus, could have been the guarantor of the Jesus tradition for future generations. In particular as apostles, they could establish future directions for the developing Church.

■ Paul and Apostles[16] ■

Paul held a different viewpoint about apostleship. Paul had experienced the risen Lord. He had been given a mandate to be a missionary to the Gentiles. He imitated the death of Jesus in his personal life and awaited a resurrection. Paul professed to be an apostle and would not let anyone deprive him of this title. No doubt Paul admitted that Peter was an apostle and even would accept the role of the other apostles, but never without his personal claim to be an apostle as well. Since Paul was not an eyewitness, he could never rely on the words or actions of Jesus personally. Yet his conviction that he had been given a mandate from the risen Lord assured him that he could also make decisions with regard to the future development of Christianity. Paul brought to the fore the problem of Gentile and Jewish Christians and the obligations upon all. His approach would have been based on his understanding of the risen Lord rather than on any words or practices of the earthly Jesus. Paul as the innovator sought the approval of the apostles in Jerusalem. They, as guarantors of the tradition, agreed with Paul, at least to some extent.[17] When, to the mind of Paul, they reneged, he confronted Peter and followed his own interpretation. Afterward he would modify this position as he failed in what he hoped to accomplish in the writing of Galatians. The epistle to the Romans gives insights into a different Paul.[18]

PAUL THE APOSTLE

Not an eyewitness
Not a local leader or bishop
Relied on his own experience to solve problems
Maintained solicitude for churches he founded
Maintained unity with the other apostles
Maintained his own position in face of others
Established presbyter-bishops?

Like the other apostles, Paul was not a local leader or a local bishop. He founded churches and probably left people in charge when he moved on. As founder, he always had a special solicitude for the churches he claimed as his own. The apostles had a concern for the whole Church and Paul had special concerns for those he founded. Whether Paul actually ordained or established presbyter-bishops in the churches he founded remains uncertain.[19]

The New Testament never proposes that the presbyter-bishops described in the various writings and letters were successors of the twelve apostles. Eventually this group would succeed to pastoral care of the local community, as exhibited by Paul, and general care of the whole Church, as exemplified by the twelve apostles in Luke's writings. These presbyter-bishops may have been appointed by the missionary apostles, but it is not certain whether this was the case. Historically it is impossible to trace the presbyter-bishops to the twelve, but perhaps some of them can be traced to apostles like Paul. Some relationship exists between the twelve apostles, other apostles, and eventually presbyter-bishops, but the development took place slowly, with some churches having such a structure and eventually all the early churches incorporating a similar structure in imitation of each other.[20]

■ Second-Level Apostles and Succession ■

Probably Timothy[21] and Titus were disciples of Paul the apostle and so could be viewed as second-level apostles. Following the example of Paul, they might intervene in Church affairs just as Paul did. With the passage of time, they too died. With the death now of the second-level apostles such as Timothy and Titus and the need for greater organization and structure for the community to survive and flourish, the presbyter-bishops rose to the level of authority in a local community. The Church moved from a period of founding apostles, to second-level apostles, and finally to the presbyter-bishop structure. Probably this structure began as a collective authority. Various communities would have had a group of presbyter-bishops functioning as leaders of the local church. Eventually this evolved into a monarchical episcopacy in certain cities—e.g., Antioch may have had such a structure before other cities such as Rome.[22] Finally the Church developed into the present structure of one bishop having a college of presbyters around him.

The function of Paul as a missionary apostle and as one given to oversee certain communities with pastoral care can easily be assumed into the office of bishop. Some of the other aspects of Paul's leadership—e.g., seeking new solutions to face new religious problems—probably were being handled by people other than bishops. Talented men and women have offered this service to the Church for centuries, whether Francis of Assisi, Catherine of Siena, Mother Teresa, or a host of others. Bishops have always recognized this service in the church and have availed themselves of the expertise of all such people throughout the centuries.

■ Concern for the Whole Church Today ■

How the twelve functioned in the early Church by having concern for the whole Church becomes more complicated when applied to the contemporary Church. Certainly bishops throughout the world can gather in ecumenical councils to discuss the concerns of the whole Church, such as Vatican II. National conferences of bishops also help. Both gatherings, however, can cause problems, since ecumenical councils cannot be called regularly and regional conferences only deal with the region. Roman Catholicism has settled the question with the bishop of Rome assuming the position of Peter in the care of the whole Church. For Luke, the twelve made the decisions that affect the whole Church. The bishop of Rome, the pope, the Holy Father, fulfills this function today.

■ The Successor of Peter ■

The study of early history both in the New Testament and in other early Christian writings offers no proof that Peter was ever regarded as the first bishop of Rome.[23] His function however, should continue. Peter plays too prominent a role in the ministry of Jesus and in the earliest Church to be forgotten or even judged as just one apostle among many. The gospel of Matthew saw a need for clear lines of authority and presents Peter as the rock on which the Church is built (Mt 16:18). The gospel of John recognized that Peter, and then presumably his successors, had an important role to play in the developing Church (Jn 21:15–19). Luke presents Peter as strengthening his brethren (Lk 22:32). Certainly this function need not have been attached to an episcopal city, but that is in fact what happened. The city where Peter died, and which eventually developed its own monarchial episcopacy, began to express properly the Petrine function of the twelve. Matthew, as noted (Mt16:17–18), presents Jesus entrusting the keys of authority to Peter. Luke (22:32) recounts Jesus giving Peter the task of strengthening the brethren, and John (21:15–17) acknowledges the pastoral care given to Peter by Jesus. No other city could claim the presence and authority of Peter as did Rome, and the bishop of Rome began to fulfill these gospel functions. The pope, as the bishop of Rome, acts in the name of Peter for the Church today. He also functions as head of the college of bishops.

Originally Peter functioned along with the other apostles, including Paul the missionary apostle, in dealing with matters affecting the whole Church. If today a worldwide Church proves anything, it shows the necessity for others to share in this Petrine function. The successor of Peter, however, still speaks for the whole Church, both in the name of Peter and in the name of Jesus. To truly continue this Petrine function demands both approaches. The pope is first the bishop of Rome joined with other bishops. He also speaks for the Church and exercises his ministry as both sign and cause of Church unity in governance.

■ Infallibility[24] of the Pope ■

No discussion of apostolicity, with its grounding on the transmission of the truth, can be complete without some consideration of infallibility. People need to feel secure in what they have been taught and how this affects their relationship to God. Truths, doctrines that are essential to faith, cannot change based upon personal or common opinion. Within the Roman Catholic tradition the teaching on infallibility has provided this necessary assurance.

During the First Vatican Council in 1870, the assembled fathers declared in the dogmatic constitution *Pastor Aeternus* that the pope under certain conditions can exercise "the infallibility with which the divine redeemer willed his Church to be endowed in defining the doctrine concerning faith and morals."[25] Previously this unfinished council[26] had also spoken of the papacy as a divine institution, with a primacy of jurisdiction over all churches, pastors and believers.

No doubt this council was affected by the historical currents of the times. Europe had experienced both the French Revolution and the rise of Napoleon. Italy had experienced an antipapal and anticlerical attitude. The enlightenment had affected all scientific study. German romanticism had called into question many of the older tenets of both theology and philosophy. Where the Church would fit in this new world structure needed to be delineated, and a strong papal authority in all matters would help. So believed many of the bishops at the First Vatican Council, even if not all.[27] While the discussions never were completed, four conditions were affirmed to be necessary before a pope would pronounce infallibly:

1. the pope acts as supreme pastor and teacher of all Christians;
2. he uses his authority as the successor of Peter;
3. the subject matter concerns faith and morals, i.e., doctrine expressing divine revelation;
4. he expressly indicates that the doctrine must be held by all.

Moreover, the declaration also states that these definitions are "irreformable of themselves and not because of any consent of the Church."[28]

The Second Vatican Council adds to the teaching on infallibility by stating that

> the whole body of the faithful who have an anointing that comes from the holy one (cf. 1 Jn 2:20 and 27) cannot err in matters of belief. This characteristic is shown in the supernatural appreciation of the faith of the whole people, when, from the bishops to the last of the faithful, they manifest a universal consent in matters of faith and morals.[29]

■ Infallibility and Divine Institution[30] ■

Are the papacy and infallibility of divine institution? Much depends on what divine institution means. The study of the New Testament offers no proof that Jesus established the papacy nor even that he established Peter as the first bishop of Rome. The references already mentioned in Matthew, Luke and John, however, point to some divine foundation for the Petrine function. These references offer some foundation for both papacy and infallibility but do not declare a divine institution of both.[31]

The modern papacy developed over a period of two thousand years and still evolves. More influence comes from the role and trappings of medieval monarchs and a reaction to Protestantism for the papacy than any foundation in the New Testament. The bishop of Rome expresses in his office a combination of elements from the earliest period of Christianity down to the influence of modern technological society. In a time when communication took years between Rome and the United States, for example, the influence of Rome and the papacy on a local church diminished. When modern communication is instantaneous, the influence increases.

The Petrine function has been attached to the city of Rome and one person, its bishop. But nothing prevents this function from changing and developing depending on the needs of the universal[32] Church. The function should be institutionalized but can change as the Church changes in history. What the present pope has done to make the Church more aware of its worldwide dimension will surely influence how future popes will fulfill the Petrine function. The Church will always need an authentic and functioning teaching office. The bishops with the pope fulfill this role. The Church will also always need jurisdiction. Someone has to be in charge of what often was and is an unruly group of believers. As sign and cause of unity in the Church, the successor of Peter continues to confirm the faith of a Church scattered throughout the world in every culture and in every nation. Infallibility falls within this general norm of the role of the bishop of Rome.

Pope Paul VI certainly knew of the Catholic teaching on infallibility. He also knew some of the problems associated with the teaching. In *Mysterium Ecclesiae*[33] Paul VI seems to imply that dogmas are historically conditioned. Does language always remain the same? Is a vernacular translation of Greek or Latin the same? Can content remain the same with a change in form? All such questions remained unanswered in any definitive way. All cause problems for infallibility. Whatever negative notions are associated with the term, it implies something positive. Because Jesus is present in the Church and because the Holy Spirit guides the Church, no possibility exists for the Church to ever fall away from the truth of Jesus Christ. Much may change but that can never change.

How can the pope teach apart from the rest of the Church? What has happened to the continuing function of the twelve other than Peter? Does infallibility involve what is believed by the faithful in the Church or what is believed by a segment? All such questions remain discussed within theology and Church law. Vatican I and Vatican II have not resolved all of the theological issues associated with the role of the bishop of Rome and in particular the meaning of infallibility. The dialogue continues.

Ordinary infallibility belongs to the Church when bishops, who individually are not infallible, do proclaim infallibly the doctrine of Christ when, "even though dispersed throughout the world but preserving the bond of unity among themselves and with Peter's successor, in their authoritative teaching concerning matters of faith and morals, they are in agreement that a particular teaching is to be held definitively and absolutely."[34] The pope also can exercise his ordinary magisterium and teach infallibly even without the formal declarations as stated above. Just when and how have yet to be determined.

Infallibility raises too many unanswered questions. No doubt some future council of the Church will discuss the issue completely. In the meantime the faithful members of the Church can rest assured that the Church will never teach anything that could be harmful to faith or to salvation. The presence of the Holy Spirit guarantees that.

■ Jurisdiction[35] ■

Jurisdiction always causes problems. Jurisdiction means universal, ordinary and immediate, supreme and full legal control. Certainly monarchs had such jurisdiction over their subjects. Historically this became the analogy for papal jurisdiction. Originally Rome claimed jurisdiction only for the western Church. The eastern Church always had its own jurisdiction. Even for those eastern churches in union with Rome, certain limitations are placed on the jurisdiction of Rome over them. Recently Rome seems more concerned for the eastern churches to maintain their distinctive qualities of liturgy, spirituality, theology and law.

Whether jurisdiction should even be used in reference to the pope and Petrine function, however, remains debatable. A sacramental primacy or a charismatic primacy, a first in rank of honor among equals—all might be better than the term "jurisdiction." Yet some jurisdiction must prevail. The Church will continue to deal with changes in jurisdiction and in the understanding of jurisdiction. Jurisdiction is not an essential aspect of Christianity, but as a human institution the Church will always have the question of containing and dealing with it. How jurisdiction functions with Rome and the Roman curia in relationship to the many churches within the Catholic Church and the thousands of dioceses presents an apparent labyrinth. In the meantime, the Church continues to function and flourish.[36]

No doubt problems of apostolicity have not been resolved completely after two thousand years. What remains true, however, is the continuity in teaching and in life. Christians today live in the same tradition as the early Church, The teaching of the apostles continues. What will happen in future years, especially with regard to the Petrine function, remains unknown. Somehow it will continue, all under the guidance of the Holy Spirit.

Study Questions

1. The Church rests upon the apostles. What does this mean to you?
2. Apostolicity is not the same as apostolic succession. Explain the implications for this statement, especially for ecumenism.
3. Compare and contrast Luke and Paul with regard to apostles.
4. What functions did apostles fulfill in the early Church? How does this continue and what are the implications for the college of bishops?
5. The pope is the successor of Peter. In what sense?
6. What does infallibility mean to you? Explain the strengths and weaknesses associated with this teaching.
7. Is the office of the pope of divine origin? Explain.
8. Does jurisdiction help or hinder the contemporary Church?

Notes

1. *Lumen Gentium*, n. 24.
2. Volume 21, n.2 of *Louvain Studies,* Summer 1996, is devoted to apostolic succession. See in particular G. O'Collins, "Did Apostolic

Continuity Ever Start? Origins of Apostolic Continuity in the New Testament." "In this sense of continuing to be apostolic in faith and life, apostolic succession is an attribute of the whole Church and is wider than episcopal succession" (152).

3. Cf. R. Brown, *Priest...*, 44–45.

4. Cf. *Baptism, Eucharist and Ministry,* 34, Faith and Order Paper 111 (Geneva: World Council of Churches, 1982). See also C. Gromada, "Toward a Theology of Ministry: The Lima Document and Roman Catholic Theology," *Louvain Studies*, Vol. 15 (1990), 354–369.

5. The overriding concern for any of these discussions involves the validity of orders within the various Christian churches. A broad notion of Catholicity and apostolicity gives a better foundation for the discussion of the validity of all Christian orders.

6. Cf. *Adv. Haer.* III, 3, 1.

7. The role of national conferences is under debate in Rome but not necessarily in the United States. Over the past twenty-five years the American bishops have regularly taught authoritatively on such matters as nuclear disarmament, the economy, evangelization, right to life, etc. These documents are accepted by the American Catholic Church as coming from the American bishops and not just an opinion of one bishop. They always teach in accord with Rome, which assures the sense of apostolic succession not only in the United States but throughout the world.

8. Cf.Brown, *Priest...*, 47–73.

9. The references in tradition about the various apostles being both missionaries and heads of local churches come from the second and third centuries. Cf. Brown, *Priest...*, 52.

10. Acts 1:13–14 clearly distinguishes the twelve from the brothers of the Lord. Cf. Brown, *Priest...*, 52.

11. The emergence of a single bishop in Rome probably did not arise until the middle of the second century. Linus, Cletus and Clement were probably prominent presbyter-bishops but not necessarily monarchical bishops. That Peter was the first bishop of Rome and founded the Christian church there can be traced back no earlier than the third century. Cf. O'Connor, *Peter...*, 207. See also Brown, *Priest...*, 53–54.

12. Cf. Brown, *Priest...*, 55.

13. Ibid., 56–59.

14. Ibid.

15. Ibid. "The group of Jewish sectarians at Qumran responsi-

ble for the scrolls had a form of community government remarkably like what Luke describes in Acts 6 and 15" (58).

16. Ibid., 59–72.

17. Ibid., 60–61.

18. Cf. O'Grady, *Pillars...*, chapter 3.

19. Some use the pastoral epistles as a sure demonstration of the passing of sacramental power from Paul to Timothy and Titus (2 Tim 1:6; 1 Tim 1:14; 5:22; Tit 1:5–7). The majority of New Testament scholars, however, do not recognize these epistles as authentically Pauline. They reflect a later period of Christian history, and they should not be used as if Paul actually ordained any of his followers. Timothy is presented as a companion of Paul in Philippians 1:1, which may have encouraged the author of the pastorals to write them as if Paul was writing to Timothy. Cf. Brown, *Priest...*, 63ff.

20. Cf. Brown, *Priest...*, 72–73.

21. This would explain the reference in Phil 1:1.

22. Cf. Brown, Meier, *Antioch...*, chapter 4.

23. Brown, *Priest...*, 79.

24. Infallibility means the inability to err and not the freedom from sin or moral imperfection. The literature on infallibility in the past twenty-five years has been immense. H. Küng began this new inquiry with his: *Infallible? An Inqu*iry? (New York: Doubleday, 1971). Rahner offers his criticism of Küng in "A Critique of Hans Küng," *Homiletic and Pastoral Review,* Vol. 163 (1971), 10–26. For a review of the various reactions to this question and in particular Küng's position, see M. Rebeiro, "The Ongoing Debate on Infallibility: Hans Küng's Contribution," *Louvain Studies,* Vol. 19 (1994), 307–331. Rebeiro not only presents Küng's contribution but numerous critiques, including Rahner, Congar, Lehmann, Lohrer, Baum, etc. Ordinary magisterium and infallibility have also raised considerable debate. See G. Grisez and F. Sullivan, "The Ordinary Magisterium's Infallibility," *Theological Studies,* Vol. 55 (1994), 720–738.

25. Often many will state that the pope is infallible. The First Vatican Council did not make such a declaration. Rather, the council related the infallibility given to the Church through the pope. Infallibility is not a personal attribute of the pope but rather a quality that belongs to the Church, given by the Lord, and the pope may exercise this attribute on behalf of the Church in deciding major issues of faith and morals. Cf. "Infallibility I and II," *Commonweal,* Vol. 123, 2 (1996), 8–10.

26. The efforts to unify Italy were happening at the same time, and since this involved the loss of the papal states, the council never

finished its task before the city of Rome and the papal states fell to the forces of Italian politics at the time.

27. One of the great debates that caused disagreement and the presence of a minority opinion regarded the role of the episcopate in formulating doctrines of faith. When it became evident that the majority were determined to assert a strictly monarchical version of papal supremacy and to exclude any phrase that would suggest any limitation (known as Gallicanism), the minority quietly left Rome. Two remained to vote no, Luigi Riccio of Italy and Edward Fitzgerald of Little Rock. See J. Hennessey, *The First Council of the Vatican: The American Experience* (New York: Herder, 1963), 273–283, and M. O'Gara, *Triumph in Defeat: Infallibility, Vatican I and the French Minority Bishops* (Washington: Catholic University Press, 1988). Also R. Costigan, "The Consensus of the Church: Differing Classic Views," *Theological Studies,* Vol. 51 (1990), 25–48. The "Ultramontanes" at the council considered that the Roman pontiff was an absolute monarch with the fullness of ecclesiastical jurisdiction residing in him alone. From him, they believed, a certain portion flowed to the individual bishops. This extreme position is matched by another that denied any real primatial authority to the Roman pontiff. As might be expected, there was also a middle position, which maintained the primacy of the Roman pontiff in certain clearly limited terms. For many this was the Gallican position. See Costigan, 31–33.

28. This was contrary to the French opinion proposed by some, which held that papal opinions are infallible only if then ratified by the Church. Since the source was the Holy Spirit, no other ratification was needed. A good summary of the issues can be found in H. Fries and J. Finsterholzl, "Infallibility," *Sacramentum...,* 132–138.

29. *Lumen Gentium,* n. 12.

30. Cf. K. Rahner,"Reflection on the Concept of 'Ius Divinum' in Catholic Thought," *Theological Investigations*, Vol. 5 (Baltimore: Helicon, 1966), 219–243.

31. These matters have already been discussed under the biblical foundations for the Church.

32. Archbishop John Quinn, retired archbishop of San Francisco, suggests some areas of possible change in his address at Oxford, June 29, Cf. 1966. *National Catholic Reporter*, Vol. 32, n.34, July 12, 1966, 13–14. Cardinal Joseph Bernadin also suggests some areas for discussion in his "Called to be Catholic," *America,* Vol. 175, n. 5, August 31–September 7, 5–9.

33. Paul VI, 1973.

34. *Lumen Gentium*, n. 25.

35. The problem of jurisdiction remains unclear. Cf. A. Dulles, "Toward a Renewed Papacy," *The Resilient Church* (New York: Doubleday 1977). Also cf. J. O'Grady, *Disciples and Leaders* (New York: Paulist, 1991), Appendix.

36. This question is also discussed by Archbishop Quinn. Cardinal Bernadin calls for a discussion of the place of collegiality and subsidiarity in the relationship between Rome and the American episcopacy.

■ PART IV ■

The Mission of the Church

What constitutes the Church? What is the Church actually supposed to do? What goals, what purpose, what direction should the
Church take at all times and places? How does the Church function
in the contemporary world?

Above all, the Church evangelizes. The Church proclaims the
gospel, the good news of salvation in Jesus Christ. To those who
have not heard the good news, the Church proclaims the saving
presence of God in Jesus. To those who have already heard and
responded, the Church continues to strengthen the awareness of
God's saving presence.

Evangelization takes place through preaching and offering
service to all of humanity. The Church can evangelize, however,
because the Church has established a communion of its members
through its offering of worship. Like the four marks of the Church,
the fourfold mission of the Church—preaching, service, establishing
a communion and offering worship—is interrelated. The Church
proclaims the word of God and offers service to humanity as a worshiping community.

Evangelizing, preaching and living the word and sacrament
demand a community. The Church as community extends itself outside of itself and yet fulfills its internal function of worship. When
people of faith come together they recognize the presence of God
within themselves and receive the mandate and the power to extend
themselves to others in service.

The Church serves humanity only because of its call to proclaim and recognize God's saving presence within. United in its members, it gathers courage and strength to serve from the common faith. The Church gives to others in its service and receives. In its service to humanity, the Church liberates from every oppressive situation, promising future salvation and present awareness of God's goodness and nearness.

The community founds its unity on listening to the word of God and celebrating worship. On a regular basis the community gathers and supports all of its members. A *com-union* exists not only on the spiritual level but on the personal and social level. The community enjoys each other's company. Evangelization forever includes greater interaction of culture and diversity within the one community of faith. With this power the community reaches out.

The worship of the Church presupposes the spiritual sacrifice of a good life. By serving others the community brings to its worship a fitting human offering to join to that of the one offering of Jesus. Nowhere is the community more fittingly expressed than in the common worship and offering of the eucharist. The word is heard, the people are united, the service of humanity joins in the one offering of the Lord to the one God of all.

The recent emphasis on evangelization[1] in the Catholic Church shows this interconnection between establishing the community through preaching the word, expressing the meaning of the community through common worship, and enabling the community to fulfill its role of service. Each dimension of evangelization presupposes the other. The Church cannot offer an awareness of God's saving presence to others unless it first acknowledges this presence in itself. This is accomplished through a constant listening to the word and praying together in the sacramental system.

The mission may be many-faceted, but in fact the mission of the Church is unified. The Church continues the one mission of Jesus, which combined the service of humanity through the proclamation of the word of God with the gathering of a people together as a community, committed to the worship of God. Each dimension needs the other for its fulfillment.

10.

Kerygma: Word and Sacrament[2]

*T*he one, holy, catholic and apostolic Church has a mission to fulfill. This Church continues the work of Jesus in every age and every place. Just as Jesus preached the word of God, so the Church preaches the same word. The primitive proclamation—Jesus died and was raised, he went around doing good, he has sent the Holy Spirit and will come again—forms the heart of the preaching of the Church (Acts 2:14–36). Thus has it been and thus shall it be. But how can this human Church continue to preach the word of God as proclaimed by the word of God Incarnate? How can humans even understand the divine word?

The Greek word *kerygma* used in the New Testament denotes both the act and the message of salvation. Often enough, English translators of the Greek word use "preaching." In many ways, however, this fails to explain the true meaning of this essential aspect of Christianity. For the writers of the New Testament salvation is inexorably linked with the "word," and the word is proclaimed in the living and dying and raising of Jesus.

■ God Communicates Humanly in the Church ■

God is word, and God becomes expressed as saving, spoken in creation, through the prophets and especially in Jesus. *Kerygma* is the proclamation of the true coming of salvation, the true presence of the reign of God in human history. This saving presence in the word brings deliverance (Acts 8:4–8), reconciliation (2 Cor 5:19), truth (Col 1:5), and grace (Acts 20:32) for all. Since the Lord Jesus himself is made present in the kerygma, the proclamation brings justification and salvation. The actual proclamation of the saving presence of God in Jesus constitutes the Church as the group of followers who hear the word of God and follow that word. The proclamation of God's saving presence is both historical and transhistorical, past and future, temporal and eternal.[3]

KERYGMA

A noun from the Greek verb referring to the function of the herald, to proclaim or to announce an event, especially a victory. The noun can mean both the act of proclaiming and what is proclaimed.

But can anyone human truly understand the word of God? Can God who is infinite communicate to creation? If God desires communication, then God must speak and communicate humanly. Communication involves more than the spoken word. Words are means of communication and are added to other forms of communication that involve ideas or experiences, events and deeds. The truly human words involve the physical, the psychological, the emotional and the spiritual. The same must be true if God communicates with humanity.

Since this work involves the Roman Catholic Church, then although the word of God is not confined to the Church, the scope remains centered on the Church. Within the Church, the word of God is heard, believed, preached and affirmed and witnessed. The Church, however, itself also hears the word of God. God speaks within the Church and to the Church. The Church both offers and receives. The word of God in the Church is also spoken to the Church and heard and believed in the Church.

■ Word and Sacrament ■

At the outset of the study of the word of God the relationship between the word of God believed and preached and the word in sacrament must arise.[4] Any inquiry into the word of God results in an inquiry into the sacramental system. Both are so intertwined that any believer can ask what makes them alike and what makes them different.

Certainly both word and sacrament constitute the Church. The power to preach the word of God with the authority of God and Jesus Christ and the right to administer the sacraments to all people are really the two basic powers and functions of the Church. Both come from Jesus and take their strength from the ongoing presence of the Holy Spirit. Since the Church exists as the sign of the saving presence

of God in human history, continuing the mission of Jesus, then word
and sacrament belong together. When Martin Luther referred to the
Church as the place where the word of God is preached and the sacraments rightly administered, he followed a long Christian tradition.
Augustine himself remarked:

> Take away the word and what is water but water; the
> word is joined to the element and the result is a sacra-
> ment, itself becoming in a sense a visible word as well.[5]

The renewed interest in the study of the Bible as God's word as
constitutive of the Church continues to demonstrate an understanding of how God continues to speak to people. The renewal as well of
preaching based on the word of God supports this approach. The living, efficacious, mighty and creative word of God has its effect. It
goes out and does not return empty.

> For just as from the heavens the rain and snow come
> down and do not return there until they have watered the
> earth, making it fertile and fruitful...so shall my word be
> that goes forth from my mouth; it shall not return to me
> void but shall do my will, achieving the end for which I
> sent it. (Is 55:10–11)

In history the revelation of God has taken place through the
word expressed in creation, made a pinnacle in humanity and perfected definitively in the incarnation of the word made flesh in
Jesus of Nazareth. No understanding of God's word can exist without also understanding the saving power of this word. God brings
about whatever God wishes, and salvation, like creation, is accomplished by God's word.

■ Intrinsic Symbolism ■

The teaching on intrinsic symbolism, important for the understanding of the unity of the Church, also figures significantly in the
study of word and sacrament. The symbol contains the reality it
expresses even if not completely.[6] Words can be symbols, but in a
special way the word of God is the symbol of God the Father as Jesus
is the symbol of the word of God, as the Church is the symbol of
Jesus, and as both word and sacrament are symbols of the Church.[7]
The reality expressed in the word actually finds its expression in the
symbol and invites participation even if the reality always remains

above and beyond its expression. God is more than the word. The word is more than Jesus of Nazareth. Jesus is more than the Church. The Church is more than its expressions. Yet each one leads back to the preceding and allows the reality to be truly present.

■ The Word Symbolizes the Saving Action of God in History ■

God wills the salvation of all people. This faith statement grounds Christianity universally and helps make the Church Catholic. God has freely chosen and freely has offered a saving presence to all. God has done this first in creation, especially in humanity, then in Jesus and finally in the Church. Jesus has entrusted his word to the Church giving to the Church the responsibility to make the message contemporary to all ages precisely as the saving word of God. Salvation exists continually in history as a creative action of God that renews a person interiorly with the individual responding in faith, hope and love. Even this acceptance, whether understood as enlightenment or inspiration, has its foundation in God's offer, but still the person has to accept. A gift can be accepted only if someone opens up the hands. God speaks internally to a person and desires acceptance. For some this might appear sufficient. In fact, it is not. The internal offering of the relationship needs some external expression.[8] The spiritual interplays with the material and the individual exists in a social context. As people live in community, the awareness of God and God's offer also involves a social event historically transmitted. The internal word offered to a person finds its historical expression in creation, in Jesus in a definitive way, and finally in the Church.

■ The Word as Saving Event ■

The word of God brings what it affirms. The word is a saving event making God present to the individual. God reveals through the word becoming present to those who hear and believe. Such a word must be understood as more of a proclamation than a teaching. Certainly, as in all religious experience, some knowledge is present; a noetic content also accompanies the word, but the emphasis remains on the actual proclamation. As proclaimed the word becomes ever more powerful.

When someone calls another by name, the very proclaiming of the name makes the event more powerful than just calling a person without using a name. Poetry is always better proclaimed[9] than read silently precisely because the power comes from the expression. No wonder that much of the Bible was written first in poetry. Those passages easiest to commit to memory are also poetry. The word of God needs to be proclaimed and the Church makes the proclamation.

■ The Word Proclaimed Differently ■

Not every moment of the Church's life expresses in the same degree or the same way the word of God. Varying degrees of intensity and concentration characterize the word, and also the power often depends on the occasion within the life of the individual or the community.

The proclamation of the word of God in St. Peter's Basilica on June 29, 1995 with both pope and patriarch present more intensely expressed the presence of God than a quiet morning celebration in a rural community. But if this quiet celebration in rural life was also to mark the baptism of a newborn or the return to the Church of someone who had been absent for years, the intensity and concentration for the individuals involved may have been equally as significant for those present in the rural Church as for the participants at St. Peter's in Rome.

■ Truth ■

Truth may be one, but how truth has been and continues to be articulated differs significantly. The same must be true for the proclamation of truth in the Church. Sometimes the Church expresses itself in a full and radical realization; other times, the Church proclaims provisionally. The same pertains to the word of God as preached in the Church. The presence and proclamation of the presence of God in the Church differs according to time and place and circumstances. Ultimately the individual responds in a complete way to the offer of God's saving presence, but since everyone lives historically, people experience God in intervals and in stages of growth. If the word of God exists historically, then the word shares in the historical process. The word grows and develops, becoming what it always was and will be. The word of God exists with varying degrees of intensity just as it comes in various ways within scripture. The word of God speaks prophetically, teaches, exhorts, instructs, edifies, consoles, persuades, announces, judges, offers testimony, recalls. The word becomes most intense especially when the word becomes joined to the sacramental life of the Church.

■ The Sacramental Word[10] ■

Over the centuries many have offered definitions or descriptions of a sacrament. The most traditional learned in the catechism still offers help in understanding: A sacrament is an outward sign instituted by God to give grace. The new *Catechism* offers something similar:

> The sacraments are efficacious signs of grace instituted by Christ and entrusted to the Church by which divine life is dispersed to us.[11]

Some years ago Karl Rahner offered his own description of the sacraments, relating them to the word of God:

> The supreme realization of the efficacious word of God as the coming of the salvific action of God in the radical commitment of the Church, that is, as the Church's own, full actualization, in the situations decisive for the individual's salvation is the sacrament and only the sacrament.[12]

Usually Roman Catholic theology distinguishes between matter and form in its understanding of a sacrament. The matter is the element used and the form is the words. But both are intrinsically united. Even the sacramental action has the element of the symbol or the word since it contains and reveals something else. The whole sacrament, everything involved, becomes an efficacious word addressed to the individual. Certainly the decisive element of the sacrament is the word. Sacraments involve the sacred as well as the profane, and the word proclaimed makes evident the presence of the sacred. The human word can offer the possibility of making the transcendent evident. Just pouring water or just passing around some bread and wine needs to be interpreted. The pouring becomes baptism when the words are added: "I baptize you in the name of the Father and the Son and the Holy Spirit." The bread and wine become sacraments when the words are added: "This is my body. This is my blood which is given for you."

■ Sacramental Efficacy ■

The *Catechism,* following the Roman Catholic tradition, stresses the efficaciousness of the sacraments. Something similar can be said of the efficacy of God's word. The biblical tradition clearly teaches the efficacy of the word, and this has long been part of Catholic theology. Something more must be added to understand the difference between God's powerful word bringing salvation and the sacraments as signs, symbols, of this same saving will.

Rahner combines the actualization of the Church at moments critical for salvation to describe a sacrament. Such a description views the Church as primary sacrament,[13] although in fact the primary sacrament remains Christ. The Church flourishes in human history as the permanent symbol that God offers grace and accomplishes grace within the life of an individual. The world has been saved and redeemed through Jesus. Perhaps the history of salvation remains open for any individual but salvation has been decided for humanity. The Church historically proclaims this victory in its very being. The sacramental system expresses and contains this reality: the saving presence of God in human history.

■ The Sacraments in an Individual's Life ■

The relationship between the seven sacraments and the life of an individual believer also offers its own significance. Each sacrament involves moments decisive for a person. Entrance into life and sickness as the foreshadowing of the end of life are decisive. Living the life of a Christian under the guidance of the Holy Spirit, making a life commitment to another, and functioning as servant and leader within the Church are also decisive. Finally, celebrating regularly the presence of Christ in a sacred meal and being reconciled after alienation are also significant moments in any believer's life.[14]

THE SEVEN SACRAMENTS

Baptism: entrance into the Church
Confirmation: living under the guidance of the Holy Spirit
Penance: reconciliation after failure and sin
Eucharist: nourishment for daily life
Anointing of the Sick: the awareness of approaching death
Matrimony: the life commitment to another
Orders: the commitment to serve the Church as minister

The word lives in the Church in various degrees of intensity. The reading of the scriptures, the mission of the Church for the poor, the teaching that takes place in home and in schools—all can be the means by which God's saving presence becomes tangible. But the fullest realization of the powerful word of God in the Church takes place when the Church expresses its being, the saving presence of God in human history at moments when an individual needs to believe in God's presence the most.

■ The Word and the Eucharist[15] ■

The eucharist perdures in the Church as a most decisive word since it expresses the presence of the very word of God incarnate. The event of salvation takes place. In the eucharist the Church remembers the past, the death and resurrection of Jesus, proclaims his presence in history now, and looks forward to the fullness of salvation for all in the future.

> *O sacrum convivium in quo Christus sumitur,*
> *recolitur memoriae passionias eius,*
> *mens impletur gratiae et futurae gloriae.*

> O sacred banquet in which Christ is received,
> the memory of his passion is recalled
> the mind is filled with grace and future glory.

■ Accepting the Word ■

God gave the word to the world in Jesus, and through the celebration of the Eucharist individual believers as members of the community accept this word in their own time in history. The Church is fully realized in the eucharistic celebration.[16] The divinely accepted act of redemption, the cross and resurrection of Jesus, becomes present in the celebration. When people hear and believe this word they experience this saving presence and the Church fulfills its destiny. All other sacraments, all sacramental aspects of the life of the Church, even the proclamation of the scriptures, become intertwined and joined to the celebration of the eucharist. Every word of exhortation, of teaching, of believing and accepting and trusting—all make one realize that God has entered into human history in Jesus and that Jesus has redeemed this world and offered salvation to all. The eucharist expresses this in its ultimate form.

> The other sacraments, like all ministry in the Church, and every apostolic work, are connected with the holy eucharist and directed toward it as their end. The eucharist, more-

over, contains the Church's entire spiritual treasury, that is, Christ himself.[17]

The bread and wine mean little without the clarifying word. The mystery of faith, "Christ has died, Christ has risen, Christ will come again," brings reality to bread and wine and transforms human elements into the vessels of the divine. From the proclaiming of the scriptures through the homily and the preparation of the gifts to the words of institution—all are realized when the individual stands and receives the body and blood of the Lord and expresses faith, "Amen! I believe!"

■ The Church Proclaims the Word ■

God's saving presence in the word exists in human history. It always did. But with Christ this saving act of God has become tangible, historical and definitive. The Church continues this proclamation of redemption and salvation, and never more so than through the eucharist. The one word of God, with its varying degrees of concentration and intensity, reaches a climax when the Church proclaims the death of the Lord until he comes in glory.

The Church continues its mission of preaching the word of God. Through this word the Church began and through the same word the Church grew. In many ways, nothing has changed over two thousand years. The word of God incarnate continues to call people to salvation in the Church today as Jesus did in his ministry and in the early Church. The same word perdures in the preaching of the Church, but especially when this word becomes joined to the sacramental word.

Study Questions

1. What does the Church preach?
2. Can God really communicate with people? What are the philosophical problems associated with this belief?
3. If God does communicate, what are the dangers in understanding God associated with this belief?
4. Intrinsic symbolism helps in understanding theology. Can philosophy also hinder faith?
5. How would you relate preaching the word to celebrating the sacraments?
6. What do sacraments mean to you personally?
7. Is the eucharist really the center of the Christian life?

8. Has the Church been successful in preaching this dimension of its life?

Notes

1. *Ad Gentes* of the Second Vatican Council sees evangelization as implantation and adaptation leading to incarnation. Paul VI in his *Evangelii Nuntiandi* of 1974 affirms that evangelization includes working for justice and the transformation of the world. John Paul II's *Redemptoris Missio* of 1990 demands the continual mission of the Church to evangelize, to preach the gospel to all outside and to continue to preach the good news to those within the Church.

2. Many of the thoughts in this section can be found in the theology of Karl Rahner. Among the works in which his theology is presented is "Word and Sacrament," *Theological Investigations,* Vol. 4 (Baltimore: Helicon, 1966), 253–280.

3. Cf. E. Simons, *"Kerygma," Sacramentum...*, 245–248.

4. Cf. K. Rahner, and K. Lehmann, *Kerygma and Dogma* (New York: Herder and Herder, 1969), 19–24; Also, Rahner, "Word and Sacramentum."

5. *In Joan.,* Hom. 80, n. 2.

6. Cf. K. Rahner, "The Theology of the Symbol," *Theological Investigations*, Vol. 4 (Baltimore: Helicon, 1966), 221–252.

7. Ibid.

8. Cf. K. Rahner and Joseph Ratzinger, *Revelation and Tradition* (New York: Herder and Herder, 1965), 9–25.

9. Cf. Karl Rahner, "Priest and Poet," *Theological Investigations,* Vol. 3 (Baltimore: Helicon, 1967), 294–320.

10. A fuller treatment of many of these ideas can be found in K. Rahner, *The Church and the Sacraments* (New York: Herder and Herder, 1963).

11. *The Catechism...*, 213.

12. Rahner, "The Word and the Eucharist," *Theological Investigations*, Vol. 4, 265; also *The Church...*, 41.

13. Cf. Rahner, *The Church...*, 11–19.

14. Ibid. 82–117.

15. Ibid., 82–87. "She [the Church] is most manifest, and in the most intensive form she attains the highest actuality of her own nature when she celebrates the Eucharist" (84).

16. Cf. *Lumen Gentium*, n. 11. "The Eucharist is the source and summit of the whole Christian life."

17. *Presbyterorum Ordinis*, n. 5.

11.

Diakonia: Service

"For the Son of man also came not to be served but to serve and to give his life as a ransom for many." (Mk 10:45)

*T*he gospels clearly present the mission of Jesus. He was concerned with the reign of God, with people coming to faith and recognizing the presence of God in himself. Jesus taught, he healed both physically and mentally, he forgave sins and drove out evil. He gave his life to a ministry of responding to the needs of others but always in relationship to a fundamental understanding of people coming into a better relationship to God. The mission of Jesus was natural and supernatural. These two dimensions coexisted without distinction. No dichotomy separated the natural and supernatural, the sacred and the profane. The love of God permeated the love of people and the love of people permeated the love of God.

THE MISSION OF JESUS

- Preach the reign of God
- Heal broken people
- Forgive sins
- Drive out evil
- Help all in their relationship to God

The clarity of the New Testament with regard to the mission of Jesus, and even the clarity of the Church's mission in the Acts of the Apostles, did not, however, prevent confusion with regard to mission over the centuries. When Peter said in Acts 3:6: "I have no silver and gold but I give you what I have; in the name of Jesus Christ of Nazareth, walk," he demonstrated his concern for the man physically, and only after the cure did the man praise God (Acts 3:8). More recently Martin Luther King remarked:

> Any religion that professes to be concerned with the souls of men and is not concerned with the slums that damn them, the economic conditions that strangle them, the social conditions that cripple them, is a dry-as-dust religion. Such a religion is the kind the Marxists like to see, an opiate of the people."[1]

The mission of the Church cannot easily be divided into the spiritual and the social precisely because no person can be so divided. Both interact and mutually influence each other. "Sin is physical too."[2]

■ Mission and History ■

The history of the Church, however, has seen a great development and often confusion in this simple understanding of mission. Even today, some see the social mission of service as substitutive. Others see it as not really part of the official mission and others still see it as a partial mission. In the light of the New Testament, all such divisions fall.[3]

Much of theology can be understood and better explained through the study of history. With the advent of Christianity as an official religion, and with the development of medieval theology based on Aristotle and Church practice based upon contemporary political regimes, the mission of the Church took some different turns. Instead of seeing Jesus as an itinerant preacher concerned with humanity, Jesus became the incarnation of the second person of the Blessed Trinity with a transcendent mission.[4] Salvation for all became living for God now, to be happy with God forever in heaven. Eventually the mission was further reduced to living happily with God forever in heaven. If this was the mission of Jesus, then the Church had the same mission.

PERFECT SOCIETIES

The State:　purpose: the good of all citizens here on earth

The Church:　purpose: the good of all believers in heaven: the beatific vision

---

In medieval theology, which continued to influence theology into this century, the mission of the Church was based more on the differences between nature and supernature than on the New Testament. The Church as a perfect society,[5] complete and autonomous, had its own end and the means to attain that end. To distinguish the Church from the other perfect society, i.e., the state, a supernatural end was emphasized. Ultimately the Church had the beatific vision as its end. Some saw one or more additional ends, namely, the exercise of the Christian religion and the sanctification of souls, but all was directed toward the ultimate end, the beatific vision.[6]

■ Natural and Supernatural ■

This approach became more virulent with the development of the enlightenment. This modern movement concentrated on the natural, the human and the rational. Since the enlightenment rejected any supernatural revelation as the foundation for Christianity, it also rejected any supernatural goal. The Church became just one institution among many in human history with no special place or privilege. Following this period theology and especially the mission of the Church concentrated sharply on the distinction between the natural and the supernatural. Any attempt to see a social, political or economic goal as proper to the Church became suspect. Religion belonged in the Church and the clergy belonged in the sacristy.

Popes Pius XI and Pius XII both followed this strict division of the mission of the Church,[7] and as recently as *Gaudium et Spes* the fathers of the Vatican Council wrote that Christ gave his Church "no proper mission in the political, economic or social order."[8] Such an understanding of the mission of the Church seems far removed from the mission of Jesus and the early community. Both Jesus and the early Church preached the kingdom that is within and forgave sins, but also healed broken people and drove out evil.

■ Various Opinions Concerning Mission ■

Political and liberation theology have returned to this biblical mission and refuse to separate the religious mission of the Church from its mission to contemporary society.[9] As a result, liberation theology and political theology have a large number of critics, especially those coming from a theology that distinguished clearly between the natural and supernatural.

Underlying these different approaches are dichotomies between natural and supernatural, transcendent and immanent, preaching the gospel and raising the standards of human life. No such dichotomy existed in the Bible. Certainly some can go to extremes and claim that the gospel can never be preached until people live on a basic level of human dignity with social and economic needs fulfilled. But others can also err in claiming that Christianity can fulfill its mission with no concern for the social and economic ills of society.

MISSION OF THE CHURCH

- Religious mission includes the social mission.
- Social mission is subsidiary and temporary.
- Social mission is substitutive.
- Laity have concern for social mission, not the hierarchy.
- The Church has many different and separate missions.

■ Nature and Grace ■

Theology in the middle of this century challenged this approach. Henri de Lubac,[10] in particular, but also Karl Rahner[11] reviewed the traditional understanding of nature and grace from Thomas Aquinas and came to different conclusions from the prevailing understanding. Nature and grace exist integrally. Nature does not exist without the influence of grace. One historical order exists and that is a graced order. Such an approach eventually gave birth to liberation and political theology and did away with the division of the mission of the Church into a proper supernatural end and a limited natural interest.

To bring the social dimension into the religious dimension as part of the mission of the Church, theologians have introduced distinct approaches. Pannenberg maintains that the mission of the Church concerns the impact of the reign of God on all dimensions of human life but that the specific social activities of the Church are subsidiary and temporary.[12]

■ The Substitutive Theory on Mission ■

Other theologians seem to follow similar veins.[13] The Church has a social mission exemplified by schools, hospitals, day-care centers,

soup kitchens, etc., but it should function in these capacities only
when secular agencies fail to offer these services.

Such a position seems contrary to popular belief, acceptance
and understanding. Few people think that Catholic colleges and
universities exist only until the state can take them over. They
belong to the mission as such. The same is true for day-care centers
or other social agencies. Some have argued that the Church should
not have such institutions but only offer chaplaincies. Again, this
contradicts popular acceptance. These institutions belong to the
nature of the Church. So think the members of the Church.

In an effort to avoid the dichotomy between the natural and
supernatural, a theory of substitution continues the distinction and
does so contrary to what most people think. Catholic Charities in a
diocese does not exist just because the state or local government is not
doing enough. It is part of the mission to heal. Movements for just
wages or working conditions are not part of the mission just because
no one else is doing this, but precisely because the mission involves
driving out evil, and less than human living conditions is evil.

■ Church Leaders, Laity and Mission ■

Karl Rahner[14] in some of his writings suggests another alter-
native. Let the Church inspire and motivate Christians within it to
accomplish what is needed for society. The official Church, especially its hierarchy, leaves the social mission to its members. The
official Church has its religious mission and the lay person has the
secular mission. This theology underlay the Catholic Action movement earlier in this century.[15]

The chief criticism of such an approach to the mission of the
Church, however, is that this places a dichotomy within the Church
between official Church leaders and the laity. This avoids the hard
question of who has the responsibility to fulfill the mission of the
Church as proclaimed in the gospel. Does leadership in the Church
also demand leadership in the social, political and economic order?

■ Many Missions of the Church ■

Still others argue against seeing the mission of the Church as
singular, or reduced to one model.[16] This approach avoids a dichotomy
between the religious and secular, the transcendent and the immanent. The social mission becomes legitimate since it neither sees itself

exclusively as the only goal of the Church's activity nor as a goal separated from the religious dimension.

This latter position differs from political or liberation theology, which seeks to link the different dimensions of the mission. Can the religious mission of the Church be distinguished completely from its social mission? Is the Church as sacrament completely distinct from Church as servant or prophet? The answer to these questions lies in the understanding of Jesus himself. Jesus was the incarnation of the word of God. Faith demands this profession. He was also one who offered freedom to all, cared for all aspects of human life, promised salvation now as well as in the future life, and generally lived as God's human face.[17] His mission seems clear: preach, heal, forgive sins and drive out evil forces. The social mission of Jesus was not separated from his religious mission.

■ Dimensions of Salvation ■

An individual cannot be divided into the religious, the human, the physical, the spiritual and the psychological. World history also involves salvation history.[18] The transcendent God has become immanent in Jesus. The sacred has always affected the profane and the profane has always influenced the sacred. When people live in peace and harmony, on a level of social and economic life that befits someone created in the image of God, these moments of salvation anticipate the fullness of salvation to come.

Justice and freedom are God's gift to all. When people live under an unjust regime, when they are shackled by political, social or economic conditions so that they have lost their sense of the freedom of the children of God, then not only is God denied but the heart of the gospel is ignored. Justice and freedom and peace belong to and form part of the Christian heritage and part of Christian responsibility.

■ Justice: Constitutive of the Church ■

The Christian message can never be reduced simply to social, political or economic reforms, but neither can such reforms be separated from Christianity. The Roman Catholic Church has a long history of social teaching. Especially since the Second Vatican Council the Church has struggled with the precise relationship between religious responsibilities and social responsibilities. In 1971 for the first time the official Church declared justice to be constitutive to the preaching of the gospel:

> Action on behalf of justice and participation in the transfor-
> mation of the world appear to us as a constitutive dimen-
> sion of the preaching of the gospel, or, in other words, of the
> Church's mission for the redemption of the human race
> and its liberation from every oppressive situation.[19]

Since that time some have had trouble with the word "constitutive."
Does it mean essential or integral?[20] Paul VI remarked at the Third
Synod of Bishops on September 27th, 1974:

> It will be necessary to define more accurately the rela-
> tionship between evangelization properly so called and
> the human effort toward development for which the
> Church's help is rightly expected, even though this is not
> her specific task.[21]

The pope challenged the assembled bishops to work out the precise
relationship between the spiritual mission of the Church and its
social mission. The documents coming from this synod affirmed that
the promotion of human rights is required by the gospel as well as
the intimate connection between evangelization and liberation,[22]
but it also adds:

> The Church in more faithfully fulfilling the work of evan-
> gelization, will announce the total salvation of humans or
> rather their complete liberation, and from now on will
> start to bring this about.[23]

Pope Paul VI in closing the synod urged further study of how
human liberation may be emphasized without detriment to the spiritual mission of the Church, evangelization.[24] He seems to have
wished to emphasize the primacy of evangelization, which also
includes liberation.

Paul VI: Primacy of evangelization—but includes liberation.
John Paul II: Evangelization is essential and includes justice.

■ John Paul II ■

The present pope, John Paul II, in his address to the Third General Assembly of Latin American Bishops at Pueblo and in his
encyclicals *Redemptor Hominis, Laborem Exercens,* and *Centesimus*

Annus, maintains both positions: he states that "evangelization is the essential mission" and at the same time quotes the synod's affirmation that action for justice is a constitutive dimension of the Church.[25] Following Paul VI, John Paul II links evangelization and liberation based on his understanding of theology. When people live on a less than human level socially and economically, this distortion is a false image of human nature. Human nature should be viewed under the understanding of Christology. The pope also repeatedly calls for an acceptance of the option for the poor.[26] Every individual conscience should become sensitized to social and political justice. Surely his own experience in Nazi-occupied Poland and then under communism has helped these ideas form in his own theological understanding.

Whatever the differences[27] between Paul VI and John Paul II, both affirm social justice as integral to the mission of the Church. Both also try to maintain the essential mission of evangelization, of preaching the reign of God. In fact they seem to have retreated from the medieval understanding of the mission of the Church to the more biblical understanding.

■ Return to the New Testament ■

The Church still seems unsure of political theology as well as liberation theology. No doubt a development has taken place and will continue to take place in the future. Somehow the raising of every human being to a sense of personal worth and dignity must be part of the mission of the Church even while it preaches salvation in the midst of human damnation.

The Church must determine how justice and the concern for the social, economic and political dimensions of human life will be integrated into the actual living out of the gospel. The American[28] bishops have taken a lead in their statements on disarmament and the American economy.[29] Without a concern for such dimensions of American and human society, the Church often loses credibility. At the same time, to become just another social agency will cause the Church to lose its soul. Returning to the biblical roots of mission will continue to help the Church resolve this dialectic. Jesus preached the reign of God; he healed people physically and psychologically and spiritually; he forgave sins and drove out evil. The Church follows his lead.

Study Questions

1. Jesus came to serve. The Church must do likewise. How can the Church do this in your opinion?

2. Should the Church be involved with politics?

3. What are your thoughts on the mission of the Church to the world?

4. All nature is permeated by grace. If so, what are the implications of this belief?

5. What do you like about liberation theology? What do you see as some problems?

6. Do you see the value of political theology?

7. If concern for justice is constitutive of the mission of the Church, what implications should flow from this teaching?

8. Does the Church serve humanity by telling people what to do?

Notes

1. Cf. *The Words of Martin Luther King, Jr.,* selected by Coretta Scott King (New York, 1984), 66. I have a recollection of a similar quote, which ended... "is spiritually moribund only waiting to be buried." Unfortunately I cannot find the source for my recollection.

2. Cf. Ernesto Cardenale, *The Gospel in Solentiname* (Maryknoll: Orbis, 1978). "Freedom from sin and physical freedom are the same thing. To keep ourselves in poverty is a physical thing, right? And it's sin too. Then what's the difference between physical freedom and freedom from sin? Sin is physical too, and to save ourselves we also need physical things" (4).

3. Cf. Francis Schüssler Fiorenza, *Foundational Theology* (New York: Crossroad, 1985), chapter 7.

4. Cf. John F. O'Grady, *Models of Jesus Revisited* (New York: Paulist, 1994), part III, chapter 1.

5. Perfect not in the sense of holiness but following the medieval understanding of a perfect society: an autonomous institution with specific goals and the means to attain those goals. Cf. P. Granfield, "The Rise and Fall of 'Societas Perfecta,'" *Concilium,* Vol. 157 (1982), 3–8.

6. Fiorenza, 198–199.

7. Ibid., 200.

8. N. 42. The document continues: "The purpose which he set before her is a religious one. The Church is willing to assist and promote all these institutions to the extent that such a service depends on her and can be associated with her mission."

9. Cf. Johannes B. Metz, *Theology of the World* (New York: Herder and Herder, 1969). For a brief summary of liberation theology and appropriate bibliography, see O'Grady, *Models...*, part III, chapter 3. See in particular J. Nickoloff, "Church of the Poor: The Ecclesiology of Gustavo Gutierrez," *Theological Studies*, Vol. 54 (1993), 512–535.

10. *The Mystery of the Supernatural* (New York: Herder and Herder, 1967).

11. *Nature and Grace* (London: Sheed and Ward, 1963).

12. *Theology and the Kingdom of God* (Philadelphia: Westminster, 1969), 90–91.

13. Cf. Richard McBrien, *Catholicism*, Vol. 2 (Minneapolis: Winston, 1980), 720–722. Also, J. Segundo, *The Community Called Church* (Maryknoll: Orbis, 1972), 96.

14. Cf. "The Church's Commission to Bring Salvation and the Humanization of the World," *Theological Investigations* 14 (New York: Seabury, 1976), 295–313. In later writings Rahner seems more influenced by the political theology of J. Metz.

15. The same idea is present in the debate of the presence or absence of clergy and religious in political positions. The general sense seems to be to inspire lay members of the Church to fulfill such offices and let the clergy and religious attend to the spiritual needs.

16. Cf. Michael Fahey, "The Mission of the Church to Divinize or to Humanize," *Proceedings CTSA,* Vol. 31 (1976), 56–69. A. Dulles, *Models of the Church* (New York: Doubleday 1976), 95.

17. O'Grady, *Models...*

18. Cf. K. Rahner, "History of the World and Salvation History," *Theological Investigations,* Vol. 5 (Baltimore: Helicon, 1966), 97–114.

19. *De Justitia in mundo,* International Synod of Bishops, 1971, n. 5.

20. The International Theological Commission's *Human Development and Christian Salvation* suggests it means "integral." See *Origins* 7, n. 20 (November 3, 1977). See Fiorenza, 208–210.

21. *Catholic Mind* 73 (March 1975), 6.

22. Cf. ibid., 50–51, 55.

23. Ibid.

24. Ibid., 58–64.

25. The Pueblo address can be found in *Addresses and Homilies* (Washington: USCC, 1979), 22–38. The encyclicals can be found also published by the USCC. See Fiorenza, 209–211.

26. The phrase has become commonplace in contemporary Catholic ethics. It can be traced to the First General Conference of Latin American Bishops in Medellin in 1968. Pope John Paul II traces it to *Lumen Gentium,* n. 8, which observes that the Church "recognizes in the poor and the suffering the likeness of her poor and suffering founder. She does all she can to relieve their need and in them she strives to serve Christ." See S. Pope, "Proper and Improper Partiality and the Preferential Option for the Poor," *Theological Studies*, Vol. 54 (1953), 242–271.

27. Paul VI seems to imply that the social teachings of the Church have been worked out in history. John Paul II traces the social teachings to the gospel. See M. Elsbernd, "Whatever Happened to *Octogesima Adveniens?*" *Theological Studies*, Vol. 56 (1995), 39–60.

28. The theology of the social gospel is a particularly American phenomenon coming out of American Protestant theology in the late nineteenth and early twentieth century. The American Catholic Church has been greatly influenced by the general culture, and this might help explain the particular interest of the American bishops in social issues. For an ecclesiological and historical perspective see R. Haight, "The Mission of the Church in the Theology of the Social Gospel, *Theological Studies,* Vol. 49 (1988), 477–497.

29. The American most closely identified with preaching justice as constitutive of the mission of the Church is J. Bryan Hehir. For some of his ideas see "From Leo XIII to John Paul II: The Evolution of Catholic Social Thought," *Commonweal,* Vol. 118 (1991), 281–282; "Catholics Can Build on Foundation of Justice," Interview by *SALT* (periodical), Vol. 11 (1991), 10–15.

12.

Koinonia: A Communion

Biblical faith forms a community of those who believe, worship God and live and work together. Believers share a common experience of salvation begun and salvation to be fulfilled in the future. While living together they bear witness to this common faith. The Church has always lived as a com-union, a union, a *koinonia*. People are joined to God through the death and resurrection of Jesus and the presence of the Holy Spirit and are joined to each other. God has entered into a covenant relationship with people, a relationship that offers the possibility of peace and freedom and justice and love. With such a relationship with God, people have the hope of experiencing these same qualities among each other.

KOINONIA[1]

The Greek word for fellowship or communion. "The grace of the Lord Jesus Christ, and the love of God, and the fellowship *(koinonia)* of the Holy Spirit be with you all" (2 Cor 13:13).

The combination of God's grace and presence in this community and the actual practice of living as a community has always created a tension. Human responsibility in action *(orthopraxis)* and the proper understanding of the relationship to God *(orthodoxos)* can never be completely or perfectly achieved at any period of history. Over the centuries many forms of community living have developed. Some helped the sense of com-union and others hindered the actual "feeling" of unity, of being together as believers.

orthopraxis: a relatively new theological term with an ancient history. Now it means action including passion and suffering. Christians do not only contemplate the gospel but act (praxis) for the kingdom. Practice follows belief.

orthodoxos: at root the word means belief in and assent to the truths of faith. Criteria for orthodoxy have been classically affirmed by Vincent of Lerins: that which has been believed everywhere *(ubique),* always *(semper)* and by all *(ab omnibus).*

■ The Early Church as Communion ■

The New Testament Church saw itself as liberated, much like the Jews of old experienced liberation from slavery in Egypt. Once they had thrown aside the shackles that bound them, they could experience the freedom of the children of God. God had delivered them from oppression and no attempt for further oppression could ever take this away. The new community could never act among themselves in a way that could be considered oppressive to any member.

This same community witnessed to the goodness of God who called all to a similar freedom, whether male or female, rich or poor, of all races and social and economic conditions. Differences surely existed but never to the extent that what was shared in common was forgotten or overlooked.

While living a com-union the early Church also needed some sense of governance in the various aspects of community life. In a perfect human existence perhaps governance would have been needed only in a limited sense. With human life vitiated by evil and sin, governance became a necessity. The actual Christian living demanded some guidelines for people to share a common life together. Governance of the community developed, responding both to the common faith and the need for order. What they experienced, like most structures of early Christianity, rested on previous experience in Judaism.

■ Community and Governance in the Old Testament ■

The Old Testament community developed its governance differently during various periods of its history. The time of the judges gave way to the monarchy. God's rule, especially with David, became mediated through the king. Worship became institutionalized under

Solomon who built the temple. The common worship of all was also controlled by the priests and hierarchy. An established worship developed with official priests as representatives of God, similar to the way that the king represented God. People experienced national prosperity and peace. God was worshiped as a God of order. All of God's creation assumed a certain hierarchy into which all persons and things would fit neatly.

■ Prophetic and Priestly Traditions ■

The prophetic tradition and the priestly tradition along with the deuteronomic understanding of the monarchy created a tenuous balance that often gave way to control by king, court and priestly hierarchy. An additional tradition from the Old Testament, Wisdom, offered a slightly different view of how the community could and should actually function. Wisdom was concerned with what works and what does not work; what helps people in their relationship to God and to each other and what hinders this relationship. Human experience and insight into human nature gives guidance on how the community can survive and flourish.

Historically under the power of kings and hierarchy, Israel moved in three directions.[2] Concern for the well-being of the wealthy and the hierarchy led to economic and social exploitation of the ordinary believers. Secondly, an enforced social hierarchy also led to the oppression of some, especially those who felt marginalized in some way. The decision to limit the participation of the marginalized in the actual community life was always done for the good of the state. And thirdly, the institutionalization of worship controlled by king and priest often led to what might be called the domestication of God.

COMMUNITY LIFE IN ISRAEL

Concern for well-being of leaders
Social hierarchy
Institutionalization of worship

The prophets frequently criticized this order, calling on the Torah and Moses for support. They advocated equality in the presence of God, a political system of justice for all and a religion that could never be controlled and domesticated into neat forms. God could not be manipulated by those who control the social order.

The ancient people, however, did not try to do away with the establishment since this would cause chaos. The wisdom tradition[3] reminded the believer that a transcendent God functioned within the parameters of human society. A dialectic exists precisely because God truly and freely redeemed people, but people must also live out a personal response to this redemption in community. The established order and those who control that order necessarily contribute to the good of all, even if at times this same order caused problems.

■ The New Testament Community ■

The New Testament community combined a commitment to Jesus with an understanding of the community traditions of Israel. He called for not a completely new community but one that united disciples as equals, who believed that Jesus embodied God's word and that they should imitate how he lived in community. This worshiping community, united under the one same God as Israel, could experience salvation. Instead of waiting for salvation to come, this new community welcomed anyone, even enemies. No restrictions existed for membership. Faith alone was necessary. People would bear witness to God's saving love for all in the community founded by Jesus.

■ Luke ■

The gospel of Luke[4] in particular tells of Jesus wandering on the margins of the established social order, calling into question the demands for possessions and protection, broadening the meaning of family, and breaking many social customs and even laws. He fraternized with whomever he chose: sinners, publicans, outcasts. His norms would be those of his Father: the love of God and neighbor. All will be regulated and interpreted through these laws. This founded his understanding of community. People will live obediently in light of a merciful God who calls them to righteousness not for what they have done or not done, but just because God has so declared. This new community forgives people whom society ignores, welcomes the outcasts, loves even enemies and shares peace with all.

■ Paul ■

Paul's understanding of the community as the body of Christ demonstrates his firm commitment and that of early Christianity to continue Jesus' understanding of community.[5] All who depend on the redemption by Jesus are reconciled with God and with each other. The whole community, every individual, has been delivered from sin and evil and death and legalism and all that alienates from the love of God (Rom 5–8). Faith has restored the community between God and humanity and humanity within itself. Now an egalitarian society has been founded (Gal 3:23–29). The new community, the Church, is the vehicle by which God continues divine activity on earth. As the body of Christ and the people of God, the Church also continues the understanding that Jesus had of God, as well as his understanding of how the human family should live.

Of course Paul also knew the tensions created when each member of the one body exercised his or her own gift. The one baptism did not swallow up human personality. The one Spirit gives different gifts (1 Cor 12:4–13) to different individuals, all to effect different ministries for the good of the community. People could have different approaches. Some members of the Roman community saw themselves free from all legalisms. The Corinthians who had no regard for meat sacrificed to idols, and those who would not eat such meat could be united as long as all was measured by the growth of the believing community. What is acceptable to one person in faith should be acceptable to another even if the person chooses to follow a different path in practice.[6] Above all, people of faith should be sensitive to each other. The unity of the community in witnessing and in life overarches all. The love for one another will unite the diversity in the community.

Since the Spirit is within the community, the early Church experienced a transformation of relationships within itself. Any oppressive elements of human communities had no right to exist. The Spirit had accomplished a revolution of virtues, values, perceptions and especially relationships. But how this internal transformation affected the outside community seems unclear in the Pauline writings. Paul insisted principally on maintaining faith. He was not overly concerned with transformation of social institutions, provided of course no oppression existed within the Church community. Whenever he perceived internal problems that harmed the well-being of the community, he reacted quickly to correct them. Galatians, Corinthians and even to some extent Romans contain clear injunctions and admonitions.[7] For Paul the community should take on particular social structures that will best enhance and preserve the gospel.

■ Other New Testament Writings ■

Since the Church functions as the body of Christ, and as a community, a *koinonia,* believers share an equality in the spiritual, physical and material benefits of God's beneficence toward them. But in the later writings of the New Testament a shift takes place much like the shift in the Old Testament toward the institutionalization of worship and gifts. Pastoral offices, as already noted, deacons and younger ones, presbyters and overseers with a clear hierarchy replace the charisms and affect the sense of equality.

> The pastorals represent the fruit of a growing rapprochement between the more formal structures which Jewish Christianity took over from the synagogue and the more dynamic, charismatic structure of the Pauline churches after Paul's death.[8]

In Ephesians also the author regards the Church not as local and charismatic but as a transcendent community of all believers (2:4–7) whose charisms have taken the form of established teachers (4:7–12). The loss of the authority of a charismatic leader like Paul and the delay of the parousia of Jesus propelled the early communities into a respectable institution with all of the offices common to such social structures. The survival of the tradition becomes paramount. The institution of the Church ensures this survival.

■ From Community to Institution ■

The egalitarianism of the early communities quickly gave way to an institution with clearly established hierarchy and office. Members of the community were situated according to the practice of the contemporary social order. Men ascended and women descended. The movement from a household community to a social Church in the Greco-Roman period accelerated this drive. The internal tension between personal freedom and responsibility and unity and diversity usually was resolved in favor of the institution.

The inevitable development of a hierarchical Church brought blessings and curses to Christianity. One of the problems of the reformation, which continues today, is the precise relationship between a hierarchical community with clearly defined lines of authority and responsibility and a priestly order responsible for liturgy and the early free-floating type of Christian community. The same tension exists in the comparison between the gospel of John and the gospels of Matthew and Luke.[9]

■ The Survival of Christianity ■

The survival of Christianity demanded an institution[10] expressing the Jesus tradition. No one should doubt that. At the same time, the dangers of such a movement perdure from the earliest problems in Israel to the actual organization of the Roman Catholic Church. Everyone will proclaim the need for balance and interplay between personal freedom and corporate responsibility, unity and diversity. Everyone sees the need for true community and *koinonia*. But how can these tensions continue to function for the good of all?

■ The Hierarchy[11] ■

Can the Church truly be a communion, a *koinonia*, and still maintain a hierarchy? The term "hierarchy," etymologically means "holy origin" or "sacred order" or "holy domain."[12] Since the time of Denis the Areopagite it has been used to signify the order given to the Church by the Lord. On a more practical level it signified those designated to represent the invisible Lord, those holding sacred authority: deacons, priests, bishops and the pope.

HIERARCHY

In ecclesiastical legal language the hierarchy is the structure composed of those who, according to the principle of unity of head and body, are called to represent the invisible Lord; more precisely, it is, in the objective sense, the institutional order within this structure, and, in the subjective sense, the totality of those holding sacred authority.[13]

The distinction between clergy (hierarchy) and laity has persisted in Church history, and so the hierarchical structure precludes a charismatic structure in which anyone can function with sacred authority. The community lives with its clearly defined divisions and distinctions. Such a development inevitably took place as the Church settled into history. If the Church was to survive and continue its mission, divisions and distinctions with clearly defined lines of hierarchy became essential.

> That divine mission entrusted by Christ to the apostles will last until the end of the world (Mt 28:20), since the gospel which was to be handed down by them is for all time the source of all life for the Church. For this reason the apostles took care to appoint successors in this hierarchical society.[14]

The bishops are the successors of the apostles, according to both Vatican I and Vatican II. Priests and their successors historically received ordination and authority from the bishops and serve the local communities. Deacons serve the bishops in a distinct order. Each shares in the authority of Christ as head of the Church.

■ Hierarchical Structure: Constitutive ■

In Roman Catholic tradition the hierarchical structure is constitutive of the Church as the people of God with its theological basis in the sacramentality of the Church. If the Church symbolizes the invisible God through its functioning as the earthly body of Jesus, then visibly Jesus will be represented in how the Church actually functions. The visible head of the Church represents the invisible head of the Church. This demands individuals who will function as representing Jesus not only to the Church in itself but also to society.[15]

This hierarchy contains a hierarchy of orders and a hierarchy of jurisdiction. Both complement the one sacred ecclesiastical authority. The authority given in orders must be actually exercised—which demands office and canonical mission. Entrance into the hierarchy of order through ordination is irrevocable. Except for the supreme authority of the pope and the college of bishops, entrance into the hierarchy of office is through canonical mission. This latter can be lost at any rank, e.g., when a priest or bishop is deprived of his office and excluded from functioning.[16]

Hierarchy of order: bishop, priest, deacon
Hierarchy of Jurisdiction: office and canonical mission

The hierarchy of order is well known as stated above: bishop, priest and deacon. The hierarchy of office also is divided. The supreme pastoral office is that of the pope as successor of Peter. The college of bishops has succeeded the college of the apostles and has the pope as its head. Individual bishops function as the leaders of a particular church, and although they received their office from the pope, they function in their own right,[17] always in union with the pope. The pope as supreme pastor and the college of bishops need no special designation to function since they exist by their own right. Episcopal office, however, needs a decision by competent authority since it concerns a particular Church community. Any particular episcopal office derives from ecclesiastical law and must conform to Church law. The actual functioning of the office, however, with its tasks and powers, flows from the hierarchy of order and is not derivative from the primatial power of the pope. The bishop leads his diocese in union with the pope but also with his own proper authority.

■ Pope and Bishops ■

All other offices are derived from the above two, pope and bishop. From the pope come the ecclesiastical offices of cardinals, Roman congregations, curia offices, papal legates, nuncios, etc. In addition the pope appoints archbishops, patriarchs, primates, metropolitans, apostolic vicars and prefects, apostolic administrators, abbots and prelates nullius as well as heads of exempt orders of priests. Derived from the office of bishop are the offices necessary to run a diocese: vicar generals, chancellors, deans and pastors and associate pastors.

Both the office of pope and supreme pastor and the office of bishop are united in a common episcopacy. They are all ordained bishop according to the same order. The pope is not ordained pope and remains always the bishop of Rome. As a result the Church is not made up of individual churches with the local church representing a part of the whole Church but rather that whole Church is present in the local church. This collegial element connects the local bishop with the pope but also with all the other bishops of the world as members of the college of bishops.

■ Hierarchy of Service[18] ■

Vatican II reinterpreted this hierarchy to include a hierarchy of service. Bishops serve the people, modeling themselves on Jesus, as do priests.[19] This conciliar change has moved the understanding of hierarchy away from power to service. What is derived from order and office functions for the sake of the community, the *koinonia.*

The council returned to the New Testament to reexamine the nature and function of the Church. Following the example of Jesus, the Church fathers reminded all the leaders in the Church that like the Son of Man who came to serve and not to be served (Mk 10:45), so the hierarchy must serve the members of the Church community.

■ The Supreme Pastor, the Pope, Bishop of Rome ■

Many Roman Catholics assume that after the death of Peter every bishop of Rome was aware of the special authority he inherited as the successor of the chief of the apostles. The early centuries, however, do not give much evidence that the bishop of Rome always functioned as supreme pastoral authority. To explain the lack of exercise of such a universal power, apologists replied that the circumstances did not merit any intervention. Often these same apologists still believed, however, that the authority resided in the office of the bishop of Rome, just waiting to come into greater prominence. [20]

Contemporary theologians and historians know too well the lack of conclusive evidence documenting such an understanding of the role of the bishop of Rome in relationship to the whole Christian community. The earliest fathers of the Church cited to support these views, Clement of Rome, Ignatius and Irenaeus, do not offer undisputed evidence and therefore cannot be used without some reservation as already noted. To understand the eventual exercise of papal authority, however, one need not suppose that the postapostolic Church was immediately in such full possession of itself, and in particular of its structure. The bishop of Rome did not immediately assert and exercise a primacy in authority.[21] Just as gradually the Church developed an understanding of Jesus as recorded in four gospels and the various other writings of the New Testament, so gradually the Church began to understand its own structure and its authority. But all was directed to community even as the Church organized its approach to governance.

■ Central Authority ■

The need for a central authority became more evident when divisions in the Church and among the bishops made it apparent that a single sign and cause of unity for the universal Church could best fulfill the continuation of the mission of the Lord.[22] Gradually the bishop of Rome began to fulfill the ministry similar to that type of ministry that Peter fulfilled in apostolic times. Such an experience caused a rereading of the scriptures in the light of this historical necessity: the Church began to see in the bishop of Rome a manifestation of the Petrine function of "strengthening the brethren" (Lk 22:32).[23]

Today most Roman Catholic theologians and historians recognize the interplay between historical factors or anthropological needs, as well as the divine commission to preach the gospel to the whole world to explain the origin of papal ministry for the community. Many such factors—such as the place of Rome as an imperial city—contributed to the development of papal authority. The structure was not instituted by Christ in a direct fashion[24] but gradually developed. What eventually emerged in the Church stemming from Christ was guided by the power of the Spirit but also included some elements which are time-conditioned. The divine institution of papal authority exists but in a carefully nuanced and refined way.[25] This does not imply that the papacy itself is the result of merely historical processes but that these processes were part of the divine plan for the Church. The faith community can always recognize in historical and anthropological elements the will of God.[26] The papacy with its full exercise of office shares in the mystery of the Church and thus forms an object of faith.[27] The study of the origins of Christian ministry in the New Testament offers a possibility that the office of the pope may itself continue to change. The understanding of the role of governance in community and in ministry in the present world offers possibilities for further changes.

■ Monasticism and Religious Orders ■

Historical circumstances affected how members of the community actually lived out the common faith. Each person could trace the faith to the preaching of Jesus, but the institutionalization of this faith brought about different explanations and different understandings of how the faith should be lived in community. One such approach to community living was monasticism and eventually the rise of religious orders.[28]

In this new form of Christian life a spiritual and charismatic type of ministry could continue to function. Monks enjoyed an independent type of authority, often in opposition to what had come to be seen as the hierarchical and juridical authority. Such an understanding of this more freely creative ministry was more prevalent in the east and indeed continues to exist in the eastern Church. In the eighth century, especially after the monothelite and iconoclastic controversies in the east, the monks assumed more of the role of authority figures as "men of God" and exercised their ministry outside the normal channels of Church life. In the west a similar development occurred as abbots and monks created their own sphere of influence. Community continued to function apart from the juridical and legal developments of the hierarchical Church.

■ Varied Governance ■

In later developments, with the rise of many religious orders both holy men and women lived out the Christian life based on the evangelical counsels. Poverty, chastity and obedience characterized these religious movements with people living a common life. Governance of the community varied according to the times, but always the desire was to function for the good of all in service to the broader Church community.

Such a development did not create a total opposition to the authority exercised by bishops and pope, but often problems arose. The understanding of authority associated with office characterized more and more the hierarchical Church. Often the New Testament ideas of ministry that were concerned fundamentally with service and that functioned more charismatically than institutionally and hierarchically characterized the monasteries and the religious orders. One developed the sense of community involved more with the governance of people. The other tried more frequently to maintain a governance based on people equally continuing the ministry of Jesus. Both continue to function in the Church today.

The Second Vatican Council did not alter the notion of the supreme authority of pope and bishops over the Church but did claim that this authority is to be exercised as service and in a collegial way.[29] Once again the notion of *koinonia* returned to prominence. Pope and bishops will use their authority and governance but only to build up the flock and serve the community.[30] The Church has developed in its understanding of structure and governance but ultimately has returned to the notion of community and service as witnessed in the New Testament.

Study Questions

1. What does community mean to you?
2. The development of governance in the Old Testament caused some problems. Do these same problems exist today?
3. The New Testament preached an equality of all. Do you think this ever really existed?
4. Jesus invited all to belong. How is this important for the Church today?
5. Paul recognized charisms within the community. How can this promote a sense of community? How can it hinder the same sense?
6. Should the Church be egalitarian? Democratic?
7. A hierarchy serves the community. What implications does this teaching offer to the contemporary Church?
8. The pope fulfills the petrine function. How important is this for all of Christianity?
9. How do religious orders contribute to the Church as community?

Notes

1. Cf. F. Hauck, *"Koinonos,"* for an etymological study.
2. Many of these ideas are taken from W. Brueggemann, *In Man We Trust* (Atlanta: Westminster, 1978).
3. For an excellent summary of wisdom thought, see G. van Rad, *Wisdom in Israel* (Nashville: Abingdon, 1972).
4. The most complete recent commentary that contains special treatment of Luke's theology can be found in J. Fitzmyer, *The Gospel According to Luke* (New York: Doubleday, 1979, 1985).
5. Cf. O'Grady, *Pillars...,* chapter 14.
6. This is one of the many problems that Paul tries to deal with in Romans; cf. O'Grady, *Pillars...,* chapter 13.
7. Ibid.
8. J. D. Dunn, *Unity and Diversity in the New Testament* (Philadelphia: Fortress, 1977), 21.
9. Cf. O'Grady, *The Four Gospels...*
10. Institution need not imply an institutionalization. Institutionalism can cause grave problems for Christianity, as it did for the Old Testament traditions. This further complicates ecumenical relationships. See E. Gritsch, "The Church as Institution: From

Doctrinal Pluriformity to Magisterial Mutuality," *Journal of Ecumenical Studies,* Vol. 16 (1979), 448–456.

11. Any standard theological dictionary can offer some general description of hierarchy. Cf. L. Doohan, "Hierarchy," *The Modern Catholic Encyclopedia* (Collegeville: Liturgical Press, 1994), 380–381. *The Catechism of the Catholic Church* discusses the hierarchical constitution of the Church in nn. 874–896.

12. *Hieros* in Greek means holy and *arche* means beginning, origin or domain.

13. K. Morsdorf, *Sacramentum...*

14. Cf. *Lumen Gentium,* n. 20.

15. No discussion of representing Jesus can exclude the contemporary issue of the nonordination of women in the Catholic Church. The representation of Jesus by a male exclusively or not has generated considerable debate, especially the concept of *in persona Christi*. The reader can examine the debate in the following: D. Ferrara, "Representation or Self-Effacement? The Axiom *In persona Christi* in St. Thomas and the Magisterium," *Theological Studies,* Vol. 55 (1994), 195–224; D. Ferrara, "The Ordination of Women: Tradition and Meaning," *Theological Studies*, Vol. 55 (1994), 706–719; Sara Butler, *"Quaestio Disputata, In Persona Christi*: A Response to Dennis M. Ferrara," *Theological Studies,* Vol. 56 (1995), 61–80; D. Ferrara, "A Reply to Sara Butler," *Theological Studies,* Vol. 56 (1995), 81–91. The entire issue has been more polarized after the publication of *Responsum ad dubium* by the Congregation for the Doctrine of the Faith on October 28, 1995. An excellent analysis both historically and canonically can be found in R. Gaillardetz, "Infallibility and the Ordination of Women," *Louvain Studies,* Vol. 21 (1996), 3–24.

16. Whether a pope can be deprived of office is debatable. Theoretically, according to some, a pope could fall into heresy and then a council would be necessary to remove a pope from office. Others will not admit the possibility of such an event and would always exclude any superiority of council over pope.

17. This issue has been discussed frequently in recent years. For an example of how bishops function in their own dioceses and how they relate to the pope and the Roman curia, see K. Himes and J. Coriden, "Pastoral Care of the Divorced and Remarried," *Theological Studies*, Vol. 57 (1996), 97–123, especially 123. The article discusses the dialogue between the three German bishops on the question of divorced and remarried Roman Catholics receiving communion. "By exercising their rightful role as pastoral leaders in

their local churches, the three Germans have signaled that they see themselves as more than Roman legates to the local church." (123).

18. *The Catechism of the Catholic Church* places the service dimension within the discussion of the hierarchy (876).

19. Cf. *Lumen Gentium,* nn. 18, 20, 27; *Presbyterorum Ordinis,* nn. 12, 15.

20. Cf. M. Miller, *What Are They Saying About Papal Authority?* (New York: Paulist, 1983), 36–37.

21. Cf. P. Granfield, *The Papacy in Transition* (New York: Doubleday, 1980).

22. Cf. J. McCue, "The Roman Primacy in the Second Century and the Development of Dogma," *Theological Studies,* Vol. 25 (1964), 161.

23. *The Catechism of the Catholic Church* places its presentation on the role of the pope within its understanding of the pope as the head of the episcopal college (880–887).

24. Cf. A. Denaux, "Did Jesus Found the Church," *Louvain Studies,* Vol. 21 (1996), 25–45. The author discusses in detail the various opinions with regard to Church origin including the many references to various official Church documents.

25. Ibid., 161. Also cf. A. Dulles, "Papal Authority in Roman Catholicism," in *A Pope for all Christians,* ed. P. McCord (New York: 1976), 53.

26. Cf. Brown, *Priest...,* 73; also, Brown, *Biblical Reflections on Crises Facing the Church* (New York: Paulist, 1975).

27. A. Dulles, "Jus Divinum as an Ecumenical Problem," *Theological Studies,* Vol 38 (1977), 695.

28. For an historical summary of the function of religious orders, see "Priesthood, Ministry and Religious Life: Some Historical and Historiographical Considerations," *Theological Studies,* Vol. 49 (1988), 223–257. Today new forms of religious life are emerging, groups composed of men and women, married and unmarried. In France one such movement is called *Chemin Neuf. Opus Dei* is also a new form of religious life. Presently these are not congregations as such. Technically they are "associations" within the Church. What they will be in the future remains to be seen. *The Catechism of the Catholic Church* explains the various aspects of consecrated life in 915–933.

29. Cf. *Lumen Gentium,* n. 18.

30. Ibid., 27.

13.

Leitourgia: The Worship of the Church

*I*n classical Greek the word *leitourgia* means a function or work undertaken on behalf of the people. Liturgy was public rather than private in nature. In the political sense the word meant public service but clearly determined service. Sometimes this service was required by all, e.g., taxes, and other times it was required only of a special few. Ordinary service for the public would include the work necessary for public games. Extraordinary service included the preparation of the navy or money needed for war. Later in classical Greek the word changed and indicated any work demanded by law for the good of the city or the good of the people. Finally the word came to be used of any work, even private, if the work was directed to others. In every stage of development the word carried a sense of service. Occasionally the word was used referring to worship, or service due to the gods. The ultimate meaning of the word in classical Greek referred to any onerous service or a service with an obligation.

LEITOURGIA[1]

Public and not private in nature for the service of all
Clearly determined public service: ordinary and extraordinary
Any work for the common good, public or private
Service due to the gods
Onerous service or service with an obligation

■ *Leitourgia* in the Old Testament ■

In the Greek translation of the Old Testament[2] (LXX) *leitourgia* translated two Hebrew words: *sheret* and *abad*. The former means service or worship or honor and can be applied to many different people, but when the word referred to God, the translator used *leitourgia*.

Abad also meant service but service in general. When the word carried a relationship to God, the translators used *leitourgia*. When the translators used the word, it always referred to the sacred: the altar, the tabernacle, the temple, or God.

The word was not used with regard to pagan ritual by the translators. That would defile the true God and the true worship due to the one God. Also, the word was not used to refer to any cult of worship but only that of the levitical priesthood, or the worship determined by law and given to certain persons to perform as leaders of the community. These were the most noble of all of the members of the community and on them special obligations rested. Thus, in the LXX the word *leitourgia* refers to the worship due to God as performed by the levitical priests. The word refers to specific service carrying a cultic and official stamp. When the prophets used the word, those prophets were also priests, e.g., Joel and Ezekiel.

In later Jewish history the word appears in both the Old Testament and rabbinical literature to indicate a spiritual worship that is not regulated by levitical norms and not in need of external support. With the destruction of the temple and the rise of the synagogue, the cult of the word of God develops and the word *leitourgia* expresses this new development. In rabbinical literature prayer is also called *leitourgia*. In the midrash on Deuteronomy 11:13 the author remarks: "How do you have *leitourgia* in your heart? By prayer."

In the beginning *leitourgia* translated *sheret* and *abad* when they had the sense of ritual worship of the temple and the rites themselves when exercised in the temple. Later under the influence of the prophets, cult was considered spiritual worship (prayer, the reading of the word of God), and this cult was also called *leitourgia*. This meaning expands its original sense, moving beyond the domain of the levitical priesthood.

■ *Leitourgia* in the New Testament ■

The New Testament writers used *leitourgia* fifteen times. Sometimes it carried the profane meaning (Paul), other times the

---

LEITOURGIA IN THE NEW TESTAMENT

Secular sense of public service
Ritual sense as found in the Old Testament
Worship

---

ritual sense of the Old Testament (Paul), and finally the spiritual
sense of worship (Hebrews). The epistle to the Hebrews includes
usage from an understanding of the Old Testament worship and
then from the notion of priesthood and sacrifice as applied to Jesus.

In the profane sense Paul remarks in Romans 13:6:

> For the same reasons you also pay taxes, for the authori-
> ties are ministers *(leitourgoi)* of God.

The same general profane sense of service is found in Romans
15:27, Philippians 2:30, and 2 Corinthians 9:12. Each text refers to
some kind of public service.

Luke 1:23 recalls the cultural service of Zechariah: "And when
his time of service *(leitourgias)* was ended he went to his home." The
same sense is found in Hebrews 9:21 (instruments used in Jewish
rites) and Hebrews 10:11 (daily liturgy of Jewish priests).

■ Jesus as *Leitourgas* ■

In Hebrews 8:6 the author adds to the basic understanding of
leitourgia as found in the Old Testament:

> But now Christ has obtained a ministry *(leitourgias)* which
> is much more excellent than the old as the covenant he
> mediates is better since it is enacted on better promises.

The author expresses the superiority of Jesus especially when he
remarks:

> We have such a high priest, one who is seated at the right
> hand of the throne of the majesty in heaven, a minister
> *(leitourgas)* in the sanctuary and the true tent, which is
> set up not by man but by the Lord. (Heb 8:1–2)

Jesus does not stand before the Lord God but sits at the right hand in majesty. The worship offered by Jesus surpasses that of the Old Testament.

■ Spiritual Meaning: Worship? ■

The word also carries a sense of the spiritual, not to the exclusion of the external, but with an emphasis on the internal, as in Acts 13:2: "While they were ministering *(leitourgouton)* to the Lord and...fasting...." Some translate the word *leitourgouton* here as worshiping. For them this refers to liturgical action such as prayers or chants or even the eucharist. Others see the meaning as private prayer, and still others regard it as a true liturgical action, an act of worship, but precisely which action is unknown.

But if the meaning was private and general prayer, the author could have used *latreuin*. He chose not to. The presence of fasting should also be considered in seeking the meaning. The context is Antioch, and Luke wishes to show how this new teaching spread. He begins by referring to prophets and teachers. They would be the chief protagonists of the new mission. The context of the community is a liturgical service that is joined to fasting. In the midst of this action, Luke narrates the election of Paul and Barnabas. The narrative closes with Paul and Barnabas being sent out to proclaim the word (Acts 13:4–5).

For some the whole scene seems like the celebration of the eucharist. The presence of fasting, however, would militate against this, since the eucharist was celebrated only on Sunday and there was no fasting on Sunday. Certainly the reference is to some public worship. If so, this is the first time the word *litourgein* is used in the sense of public worship in the New Testament.

■ Paul and *Leitourgia* ■

Romans 15:16 also offers an important understanding of the practice of the early Church:

> ...because of the grace given to me by God to be a minister *(leitourgon)* of Christ Jesus to the Gentiles in the priestly service of the gospel of God, so that the offering of the Gentiles may be acceptable, sanctified by the Holy Spirit.

Paul is a sacred minister and his responsibilities are connected with sacrifice. The use of the word "priestly" and the reference to offering refer to sacred actions. Paul is the priest who sows the seed of the gospel in the hearts of the Gentiles and completes his work. The Gentiles become an acceptable sacrifice. Liturgy has gone from temple to synagogue to the preaching of the word of the gospel to the worship of God through which the Gentiles become spiritual offerings to God through the Spirit.

■ The Early Fathers ■

In the early fathers of the Church the word does not occur as frequently as in the New Testament. The sense of worship is obvious, however, in the *Didache* (chapter15). "Choose for yourselves bishops and deacons and they will perform *leitourgiam* for you."

In Clement's letter to the Corinthians the author used *leitourgiam* for service in general inasmuch as the winds are servants; service that the angels render to God; the service by which the saints worship God through the offering of a holy life; the service of the apostle toward the flock and the cultic service exercised by Church ministers with particular reference to the service of the bishop.

In other early writings the word means sacred service, a particular divine service such as prayer and baptism and even hierarchical office. The word comes to refer to diverse Christians rites as well as the office by which persons are placed in the hierarchy.

■ Problems with the Word "Liturgy" ■

The word "liturgy" has in itself nothing that necessarily refers to Christian worship. It came from usage in the Old Testament from the technical pagan word. The lack of a specific Christian meaning becomes more evident when one realizes that the word came into Latin translated as office, or ministry, or celebration, or sacred action.

Even the original sense of the word as meaning "public" is insufficient to use it for worship. And the sense of worship of the people also is not expressed by the word, since originally it meant service for the people and not by the people. Some would also say that the word "liturgy" connotes more the external aspect than the internal aspect.

In Church literature from the sixteenth century on, the word referred more to rubrics than any sense of internal worship expressed externally. As late as 1958 the meaning referred principally to regulations.[3] Even references to the Roman liturgy or the Maronite liturgy or the Byzantine liturgy usually refer primarily to the rites and how they are carried out, rather than the sense of worship.

■ *Latreia* ■

In the Old Testament *sheret* and *abad* were sometimes translated in Greek by *latreia* (Ex 23:25; Deut 6:13; 10:12) as well as by *leitourgia.* In the New Testament *latreia* always means worship due to God (Mt 4:10; Lk 2:37; Acts 26:7; Rom 1:9; Heb 8:5; 9:14) and carries an emphasis on the internal aspect of worship.

In the New Testament when the author wishes to contrast Christian worship to Jewish worship, then usually the writers used *latreia,* which indicates more the interior disposition of the person rather than external ceremonies. *Latreia* gives value to the ancient liturgy. Otherwise it remains purely ceremonial. In the New Testament true worship expresses the spirit, not only the human spirit but the Holy Spirit that is given by the Lord.

True Christian worship is always *latreia,* which emphasizes the internal but not without the external. The word can indicate both. The difference between Christian worship and worship of the Old Testament or pagan worship often centers on the meaning of sacrifice. The Christian does not need victims, since Christians offer themselves to God in an interior and spiritual union with Christ through the Spirit. The chief offering belongs to Christ and the Christian shares in this one offering.

With so many reasons not to use the word "liturgy," why has the word become so common in ordinary usage as well as in official Church documents? What has the word come to mean today so that it can actually express what the Church does?

■ Definitions of Liturgy ■

Historically the definition of liturgy has usually been taken from Pius XII's encyclical *Mediator Dei* (1947). "Liturgy is the whole public worship of the mystical body of Christ, head and members."[4] In this encyclical the pope rejects liturgy as purely external and ritualistic as well as the notion of liturgy as juridical. Both had been part of the traditional notion of liturgy. The encyclical also rejects the meaning of liturgy as being fundamentally an aesthetic experience. Liturgy is the worship of the Church.[5] Liturgy is not just any worship but that which belongs properly to the Church. It has its origin in Christ and in some ecclesiastic order.[6]

In this century many have struggled with descriptions of liturgy, emphasizing one element over the other. Certainly it involves the priesthood of Jesus and official ministers. The result or end of liturgy is always worship of God and human sanctification. Although aesthetics are not the most fundamental aspect, apt ritual remains important. Such is obvious in every Church ceremony.

Liturgy also involves how people live. The spiritual sacrifice of a good life belongs to liturgy. The mission of the Church, the mission of Jesus continued in the lives of his followers, forms the substance of what the Church brings to its worship of God. The one offering of Jesus includes the offering of his followers in the Church.

Liturgy involves mystery. First the worship of the Church involves the mystery of God's plan for all creation through Jesus and then it involves the mystery of how Jesus remains in the Church. The mystery also involves how the Church experiences itself and how the Church experiences the presence of the crucified and risen Lord.[7]

■ Many Descriptions and Definitions ■

In fact, *Mediator Dei* offers many definitions and descriptions of liturgy. The pope did not wish to give any final definition of what the Church does but wished to emphasize certain important elements. These same elements appear in most liturgical histories and in all liturgical theology.

True worship, true liturgy, rests first on the perfect worship offered to God by Jesus the one priest and mediator of the new covenant. This worship fulfilled the worship of the Old Testament. Jesus lived his whole life as worship of God and wished that his relationship to God might continue in the Church, inviting others to join in this one communion.

TRUE WORSHIP

The worship offered by Jesus as priest
The worship that fulfilled the Old Testament
The worship in the Church joined with that of Jesus

■ The Worship of Jesus ■

The Church functions with the task of worshiping God as did Jesus. The Lord has given to the Church his own personal worship as a continual gift. The Church worships God through the worship of Jesus, the one priest. The liturgy of the Church continues the liturgy of Jesus and joins to this one act its own desire and efforts to render appropriate service to God.

Jesus worshiped God by proclaiming the kingdom, by sanctifying himself so that others may also be sanctified (Jn 17:19). Jesus manifested the glory of God and brought about the sanctification of people. In fact, the sanctification of people renders worship to God. The service given to God is the holiness of God's people made possible through the proclamation of the gospel.

The sanctification of people does not mean a moral holiness but a participation in the saving mystery of Jesus through living as Jesus did. People are made holy by Jesus and so live the spiritual sacrifice of a good life. Moral activity flows from what people are rather than the concept that people become holy through moral activity. Jesus has sanctified his followers. This comes first.

Liturgy is the act of worship of Jesus joined to the personal worship of the Church which brings about the sanctification of people and is expressed in ritual. The principal aspect of liturgy is the worship not as social but as the personal act of Christ and then of the Church joined to Christ. Since the one true liturgy precedes the Church, the Church is first passive and then active. By receiving the liturgy of Christ, the liturgy of the Lord becomes constitutive of the Church itself. The Church is most the Church when it worships God through the continuous offering to God of Jesus. The Church offers the only true worship to God since it continues the worship of Jesus. Christ offered the true worship by proclaiming the good news to the poor, caring for them and serving them. He became the sign of salvation for all and continues this role in the Church.

■ Vatican II ■

The Second Vatican Council began its work with a renewal of the liturgy. The Church fathers began by placing liturgy in a theological and biblical perspective. Liturgy makes sense only in the context of the eternal plan of God for the salvation of all people through Jesus. This one plan God has revealed through the prophets and then in Christ, whose humanity becomes the instrument of salvation for all.

The salvation of Christ consists in the reconciliation of people with God and the worship of God completely and perfectly. In the *Constitution on the Liturgy,* the council fathers introduce the paschal mystery as a theological factor to be integrated into the full understanding of what liturgy means and what the Church does in its liturgy.[8]

■ The Paschal Mystery[9] ■

The paschal mystery of Jesus has brought liberation and salvation. Once promised to Israel, now Christ transmits this liberation and salvation through his Church to all people. The liberation and salvation constitutes the heart of the liturgy of the Church and involves the mystery of the Church.[10]

The constitution places the liturgy on the same level as the whole mystery of salvation in the incarnation of Jesus. Liturgy involves the mystery of redemption and the glorification of God and actuates God's eternal plan for all. Liturgy is the last and the eschatological moment of the incarnation under the aspect of the paschal mystery.

THE PASCHAL MYSTERY

The coming of Jesus in human form, his ministry, culminating in his death and resurrection and the sending of the Holy Spirit. Each element forms part of the one paschal mystery. Individuals become enveloped by this mystery in their profession of faith and thus are joined to the Christian community.

The ritual associated with liturgy proclaims and effects its meaning. Through this sign, God expresses the eternal will for salvation and people participate and receive salvation. The worship of Christ in his paschal mystery now involves the worship of the faithful followers.

Liturgy must not be seen as just natural worship elevated to a supernatural level. Christian liturgy exercises the one priesthood of Jesus the Christ. Liturgy belongs to the virtue of religion but is an act primarily of Jesus and then of the Church and its members.

In his paschal mystery Christ worshiped God in truth. He did not just offer a ritual. His priesthood differs substantially from all other forms of priesthood. Thus his activity differs as well. Through the sanctity that Jesus possessed he offered perfect worship to God his Father. He made himself holy and offered himself to God.

The worship of the Church contains this true worship in sign. The true worship of Jesus transcends any ritual enactment, but the heart of the worship of Jesus continues in the Church in its sacred acts of worship. What Jesus offered the Church offers.

Liturgy is the perpetual actuation of the paschal mystery in which the priestly work of Jesus through efficacious signs continues in the Church. In this paschal mystery he fulfills the promises of old, enacts the new covenant and creates the new people of God. He has moved from earth to heaven to God his Father. The redeemer has sent his Spirit as a reminder of what has already happened, what is happening now, and what is yet to come.

■ Sacred Action ■

Liturgy is a sacred action through which in ritual the priestly work of Christ, the sanctification of people and the glorification of God are exercised and carried on in the Church and through the Church. As sacred action liturgy involves not only the interior *(latria)* but an external action. The ritual empresses humanly the willingness to receive salvation and redemption. As Christ was willing to worship God through his accomplishment of the salvation and sanctification of people, so the Church does likewise.

Liturgy is instrumental, a means, not an end, and not any sacred action but one in which Christ is present as the principal agent. This sacred action participates in the actions of Jesus. The Church does what Christ wishes to be done. The Church in liturgy serves the will of the Lord.

Ritual is important. The rite signifies and effects what it signifies. As Jesus was the symbol of the word of God, so the liturgy of the Church signifies the Church as continuing the saving presence of Christ. Words and actions and things and movement and place— all contribute to the effective sign of God's saving will made possible by Jesus in the Church.

■ The Priestly Work of Christ ■

The priestly work of Christ continues. The total work of Christ was priestly inasmuch as he was always mediator and always offered himself to God. His actual sacrifice on Calvary and his paschal mystery completed what he had begun in his incarnation. Through this sacrifice Christ summed up his life. The final priestly activity constituted his holy people, his own royal priesthood. The Church continues this same activity in its liturgy.[11]

Jesus glorified God through the sanctification of people. By his ministry and his death and resurrection Jesus gave glory to God. He continues this glorification and sanctification in the liturgy of the Church. His whole life including death and resurrection are now made present in the worship of the Church.

As the body of Christ the Church becomes the place where Jesus as head of the Church functions. Because the Church is first the subject of liturgy, it receives. The priestly work of Christ moves to his Church and then people are part of this one body. Just as the eucharist makes the Church, so liturgy makes the Church. Without liturgy, the Church cannot function.

■ Christ Acts Through the Church in Liturgy ■

Christ acts now through his Church. The priestly work of Christ has become present now through the participation of the work of the Church as the body of Christ. The liturgy pertains to the Church constitutively. Through the Church, Christ becomes present in the world. Through the Church the priestly work of Christ becomes actuated in every time and place. The Church offers liturgy.

The celebration of the eucharist best exemplifies the liturgy of the Church since it culminates in the union of people with God through Jesus present in the ritual and sacred meal.[12] Liturgy also includes other expressions, in particular the official prayer of the Church and the entire sacramental system. The paschal mystery of Jesus becomes more evident to believers when they live out this mystery through the liturgical year, joining personal prayer to the official prayer of the community.

The service rendered to God in worship creates liturgy. The actual living out of the spiritual sacrifice becomes the human content added to the one offering of Jesus. Through many actions and the use of ritual and things, people become sanctified and complete the one priesthood of Christ. The community has gathered, bringing its spiritual sacrifice of service in the world, having responded in faith to the word of God, and worships as it offers the liturgy of the Church.

Study Questions

1. What does liturgy mean to you?
2. Jesus is the only true liturgist. Yes or no? Explain.
3. Are rubrics and ritual important in life?
4. What description of liturgy do you prefer? Why?

5. Liturgy involves worship. How do people worship God?

6. Liturgy involves mystery. Explain.

7. Did the reform of the liturgy in Vatican II help or hinder the contemporary Church, or both? What are some of the benefits and what are some of the problems?

8. What does the paschal mystery mean to you?

9. What happens in the liturgy in your local church, both theologically and practically?

10. Does good liturgy really make any difference?

Notes

1. A full explanation of the etymology and usage in classical Greek and the Old and New Testaments can be found in H. Strathman and R. Meyer, "*Leitourgos-leitourgikos*," *Theological Dictionary of the New Testament*... This work can never claim to be an adequate treatment on this important function of the Church. Liturgy must be situated within sacramental theology and at the same time relate to a broader ecclesiology and develop its own area of responsibility and expertise. For the relationship between sacramental theology and ecclesiology, see H. Vorgrimler, *Sacramental Theology* (Collegeville: Liturgical Press, 1992). Vorgrimler is very much influenced by Rahner, as is this author. A good introduction to liturgy both historically and theologically can be found in A. Adam, *Foundations of Liturgy: An Introduction to Its History and Practice* (Collegeville: Liturgical Press, 1992).

2. The Hebrew Bible was translated in Egypt and is called the Septuagint or LXX. In Egypt *leitourgia* meant a forced public service. In Exodus the Hebrews were forced into public service in fact. But when the translators came to translate this forced public service they used the Greek word *ergon* (work) rather than *leitourgein*. In the LXX, the latter was used only of service due to God.

3. Cf. *Instructio de Musica Sacra et de Sacra Liturgica*. Acts of worship were to be considered liturgical only if they were performed according to the regulations approved by the Holy See in printed books.

4. *Mediator Dei,* n. 25.

5. Cf. Joseph Jungmann, "Liturgy," *Sacramentum Mundi*, Vol. 3, 320–331. This same work offers a good history of the liturgical movement in this century up to the Second Vatican Council.

6. *The Catechism of the Catholic Church* treats both the theology and the history of liturgy in nn. 1066–1109. It is the work of Father, Son and Spirit within the Church.

7. Otto Casel was the principal theologian of liturgy as mystery. His theology is not always easy to follow, but it figured significantly in the liturgical movement. Some thirty years ago Casel was discussed frequently in all studies of liturgy. Now he is mentioned less frequently. For an excellent summary and critique of Casel, see "La Théologie des Mystères," *Revue Thomiste*, July-September 1957, 510–551. See also J. Lecuyer, "Efficient Causality of the Mysteries," *Theology Digest*, Vol. 3 (1955), 106–107.

8. Cf. *Sacrosanctum Concilium*, nn. 1–9.

9. *The Catechism of the Catholic Church* situates the sacraments in the context of the paschal mystery, nn. 1113–1130.

10. Ibid., n. 6.

11. "It is the whole community, the body of Christ united with its head that celebrates" *(The Catechism...*, n. 1140) "The celebrating assembly is the community of the baptized who, 'by regeneration and the anointing of the Holy Spirit, are consecrated to be a spiritual house and a holy priesthood that...they may offer spiritual sacrifices.' This 'common priesthood' is that of Christ the sole priest, in which all his members participate" (n. 1141).

12. "The eucharist is the source and summit of the Christian life...by the Eucharistic celebration we already unite ourselves with the heavenly liturgy and anticipate eternal life when God will be all in all." "In brief, the eucharist is the sum and summary of our faith" *(The Catechism...*, nn. 1324, 1326, 1327).

■ PART V ■

Conclusion

14.

The Once and Future Church

Today many people wonder about the meaning of life and in particular the role of religion and the Church. Most American Roman Catholics face the same questions. In fact, the questions almost seem more urgent as one generation wonders if the coming generation will maintain the same religious traditions and virtues and values. Do young people really accept and follow the traditions and teachings of the Church? Will the Roman Catholic Church still be around for future generations? Will anyone really care?[1]

■ Social Concerns ■

The promise of Vatican Council II all too often gave way to confusion and even mistrust. Divisions seem more apparent now than ever before. Instead of a plurality in theology and understanding and practice of faith, some want a monolith, even if such a monolith never really existed. Others seem to have little concern for history and traditions. No wonder confusion reigns and questions abound.

The decline in religious vocations and the equally alarming decline in church attendance does not augur well for the next generation. How will the Church survive if fewer people are interested in leadership in the Church and fewer attend regularly? Some are also concerned with the continuous drop in financial support as Roman Catholics give a lesser percentage of their income than their forebears and even their Protestant friends. Will there be a future Church, and, if so, what will it be like?

The recent scandals involving Church leaders also have not helped. It does little good to talk about the presence of child abusers or pedophiles in all walks of society including the clergy. It does not console anyone to speak about the small percentage of priests and bishops who have sinned publicly in sexual matters. Even if the vast majority of clergy are good and trustworthy, one case is one too many.

The troubles in American society also have influenced the thoughts of American Catholics. Whether the social ills that pit race against race, or the economic ills that pit rich against poor, or the political ills that put everyone against everyone else, all are part of the American landscape. A Church so tied in to American tradition cannot remain above the turmoil.

■ Individual Concerns ■

Loneliness, anxiety and depression also seem to be more prevalent than in the past. These maladies of spirit grow within the Church and within every level of the Church. The concern for a future that will be better than the past, an anxiety about the absence of values and the depression caused by a never-ending increase of violence must affect every individual.

Crises are no longer reserved for mid-life. Crises happen every year and every day. Just when one problem seems to be solved, another rises up, commanding attention. Just when one emotional and psychological need has been fulfilled, another seeks nourishment. Individual crises involve family crises and then societal crises, and surely religion fits right in.

■ Nostalgia for the Past ■

The early Church as depicted in Acts 2 seems so nice and comfortable:

> And all who believed were together and had all things in common, and they sold their possessions and goods and distributed them to all, as any had need. And day by day, attending the temple together and breaking bread in their homes, they partook of their bread with glad and generous hearts, praising God and having favor with all the people. And the Lord added to their number day by day those who were being saved. (Acts 2:44–47)

Of course such an idyllic picture belonged more to Luke than to the early communities. The careful reading of the New Testament, especially the letters of Paul, gives enough evidence of greed, backbiting, cheating, sexual sins, jealousies, class against class and all the other sins that never move far from human society. The early Church was as sinful as any church in any period of history. For that early period as well as for today, believers need forever to seek and find a new heart.

■ A New Heart ■

Jesus offered the possibility for a new heart by his teaching of faith and love. He carried an attitude, an approach to God and to people that uplifted rather than put down. He exercised a freedom that truly liberated his followers. He concerned himself with the ordinary aspects of people's lives and offered a hope for a better future.

The members of the Church need such a heart. God offers and the individual needs only to accept. The gospel corresponds to human aspirations of dignity and freedom and intimacy and personal worth and peace and gratitude and the hundreds of other virtues known and desired by all. The gospel does not impose anything from outside but fulfills what is coming from within.

The Church offers this gospel simply, because most people live simple lives. The common and ordinary bear the divine and not just the overwhelming and glorious. Most people live and die not as the rich and powerful and famous. The new heart promised by Jesus through the Church in the power of the Spirit makes sense to all people, on every level of society.

The gospel is also freely offered and never imposed. Individual freedom and dignity demand respect and not coercion. If God allows people to go away, if Jesus asked his disciples if they too would go away (Jn 6:67) then the Church also allows people to live their individual lives, hoping and praying but never demanding, offering the possibility of the new heart but not trying to impose it.

The witness of the Church rests on sincerity and truth. The Church in all of its members, and especially its leaders, does not pretend to be other than what it is: the servant of the Lord and the servant of all. The truth that liberates expects the acceptance of God's saving presence in the whole world offered to all people. The new heart prevails in all of the Church's activities. The Church tells the full truth.[2]

The cost of such discipleship and the seeking of a new heart never comes cheaply. An easy grace is not human since human life bears the stamp of evil and sin as well as holiness and grace. The gift of God blesses people and people repay with the gift of themselves. This costs much. People learn to live life when both good and bad, knowing that God remains present in all moments of life.

Essentials matter. The faith commitment to Jesus and the love of brethren gather disciples together, creating a new heart. These qualities also keep the disciples together in community. Nonessentials can come and go, and this can include certain Church structures, practices or even hallowed traditions. Faith, hope and love remain (1 Cor 13:13).

People, believers, always remain open to the power of God in human life. People seek God all the while God pursues them. All believers have to do is open their eyes.

> Does the fish soar to find the ocean
> The eagle plunge to find the air
> That we ask of the stars in motion
> If they have rumor of thee there?
>
> ...
>
> Tis ye, tis your estranged faces
> That miss the many splendour'd thing
>
> ...
>
> And lo, Christ walking on the water,
> Not of Genesareth but Thames.[3]

God is not dead or asleep. God is present everywhere.

The new heart helps believers to be open to the neighbor and sensitive to need. The covenantal virtues of kindness, compassion, mercy and fidelity help. The example of Old Testament saints, Jesus himself, and the millions of others, holy men and women, offers the model to follow.

The new heart encourages believers in the Church to forgive themselves. God forgives, so all can forgive even themselves. Weak people are also faithful people. God is not absent when people sin and fail. God is ever more present and forgiving.

Positive attitudes help. Freedom in law; freedom from social pressures; freedom for all women and men and children; freedom in the midst of authority and structure—all are part of the Christian heritage. Even when individual freedom may give way momentarily for the good of the community, positive attitudes toward freedom help. The new heart creates and enlivens and gives hope for all.

■ The Future Church ■

The future Church is the Church of the past based on gospel virtues. The members are a community of followers loving and supporting each other. The future Church is what the Church has always been and will continue to be: one and many; holy and sinful, catholic and limited, apostolic and the creation of the Holy Spirit.

Communication in this community functions dynamically and freely. People talk to each other. People listen to each other. Otherwise no community exists and virtues lie smothered and forgotten. The fidelity of the Bible gives birth to integrity. People tell the truth and remain faithful to that truth in all circumstances. The truth never frightens. Only falsehood in the Church can cause alarm. Gospel virtues expect people to live according to principles coming from Jesus and the Church traditions.

Gospel virtues overlook personal gain in favor of others. Self-seeking, self-concerned members of the community suffer themselves and harm the entire Church. Influence certainly continues, but based on competence and holiness, just as Jesus' influence was based on his person, his gifts and his ministry.

The early Church made many mistakes. The future Church will also make mistakes, for the past and present Church has continued the tradition. Taking a false step never causes irreparable damage, for a false step can always be corrected. The Church will never move completely in a false direction. God will see to that. This gives the Church the freedom to make some false steps and then correct them.

Individual members have always made a contribution to the whole Church from every level. This also continues. Initiative belongs to all. Everyone has talents and gifts. The Church of Corinth celebrated such differences in gifts. The Church today continues to do likewise. Responsibility belongs to being created in the image of God. The Church encourages members to accept personal responsibility for self and for the community. This gives birth to new ideas and new ways of experiencing the saving presence of God for all. A prejudice exists always in favor of people. All have been graced and all are called to the fullness of salvation in Christ Jesus. People are basically good and honest and deserve to be treated in a manner recognizing this dignity.

Above all, the Church of the future will continue to return to the sources in the Bible and tradition.[4] What the Church will be rests on what the Church is and was. Such an endeavor does not amount to archeology or a repetition of the first century or the thirteenth century. Rather, the return to sources gives a richness to adjust to every new condition. The once and future Church is the same Church based on the teaching and ministry of Jesus, the one, holy, catholic and apostolic Church, the same Church that for two millennia has proclaimed, served, gathered together all peoples and celebrated in worship the goodness of God to the human race in Christ Jesus.

Notes

1. Cardinal Bernadin recognized the questions in the Church in the United States in his list of concerns: women's role, religious education, liturgy, sexuality, image and morale of priests, laity in leadership roles, the Church and political life, the American Church and diverse cultures, the Catholic school system, dwindling financial support, decision making and consultation, the role of theology and Church teaching, the place of collegiality and subsidiarity. He calls for a discussion and confrontation of all of these issues. See "Called to Be…, *America*, 6–7.

2. In 1880 Pope Leo XIII opened the Vatican Archives for historians, and in a letter of August 18, 1883, he offered the fundamental norm of historical investigation, which fits well the attitude that belongs properly to the Church: "The first rule is that one may not dare to lie, and the second, that one is not afraid of telling the whole truth"; R. Aubert, *Geschiedenis van de Kerk*, v. 10 (Bussum: Paul Brand, 1974), 215. Quoted in L. Janssens, "The Non-Infallible Magisterium and Theologians," *Louvain Studies*, Vol.14 (1989), 247. Recently the Most Rev. Edwin B. Broderick quoted the following to me and ascribed it to Leo XIII: "Dic veritatem. Deus non indiget mendacium" ("Speak the truth. God does not need a lie"). I could not find this quotation but wish to include it. The above-mentioned article is worth reading since it gives an overview of the relationship between Rome and theologians over the past century.

3. Francis Thompson, "In No Strange Land."

4. A study of the various eras in Christianity helps to clarify how the same faith persists through the centuries. "To demonstrate that the same faith was preserved through the ages, it is not enough to know St. Thomas Aquinas and to shut oneself up in him (which in any case is an inadequate method for understanding him properly since he did not come as a sort of absolute beginning). On the contrary, it is necessary to have a thorough knowledge of the scrip-

tures, the fathers, and medieval theology.... The expression of Christian thought is always relative to a language, and Father de Lubac takes account of that part which is relative. Obviously, then, it is precisely his work which is best suited to the task of saving the transcendence of Christian revelation amidst historical evolution." Quoted in L. Janssens..., 219. De Lubac is quoted here as one who continually returned to the sources that made his theology so valuable. The return to the sources offers not only an explanation for pluralism in theology but also its value.

Index